Transforming Health Care by Leveraging Artificial Intelligence and Machine Learning

Verses Kindler Publication

Verses Kindler Publication.

Website: www.verseskindlerpublication.com

Transforming Health Care by Leveraging Artificial Intelligence and Machine Learning

By: Dr. Balasubramanian Mahadevan

ISBN: 978-93-5605-391-5

NON-FICTION STORIES 1st Edition

Price: INR 400/ $18

Disclaimer

Transforming Health Care by Leveraging Artificial Intelligence and Machine Learning is written by Dr. Balasubramanian Mahadevan.

The published work is the original contents of the author and he has done his best to edit and make it plagiarism-free.

The characters may be fictitious or based on real events but they are not meant to hurt anyone's feelings nor portray anything against any caste or system. Any resemblance of names of actual person, place or institute is purely coincidental to carry forward the story.

In case of any plagiarized write-up, the author is solely responsible for it, the publisher would not be responsible for it.

FOREWORD

The convergence of Health and Technology has opened up an entirely new frontier of medical practice, diagnosis and treatment. Artificial Intelligence and Machine Learning are very promising avenues that ensure efficiency, better patient outcomes and an optimal resource allocation.

By analyzing vast amounts of patient data these technologies help in developing predictive models to identify complex patterns and actionable insights. These models also help in a more person centric healthcare and treatment. The book written by Prof. Dr. Balasubramanian Mahadevan on **'Transforming Health Care by Leveraging Artificial Intelligence and Machine Learning'** is worth reading and applying the same to one's practice. The most important chapter of the book is to lay the foundations for specific applications of Artificial intelligence and Machine Learning in diagnostic accuracy. The cases presented in the book involve areas where Artificial Intelligence has been applied to early diagnosis especially in the area of neurological disorder, cancer, cardiovascular diseases etc. The book also refers to the various challenges that one would face in the application of Artificial Intelligence and Machine Learning especially in the areas of data privacy and security.

I am quite confident that readers will find this book not only informative but also inspiring and I am sure that the book will foster new ideas and drive meaningful and impactful changes in the healthcare domain.

Prof. Dr. R. Gopal

Director, Head of the Department & Former Dean

<u>Resume of Prof. Dr. R. Gopal,</u>

Prof. Dr. R. GOPAL is basically an Engineer from I.I.T., Kharagpur in Mechanical Engineering. Subsequently, he did his MBA, ICWA, PhD and Post-Doctoral Research degree -- D. Litt. Currently, Dr. R. Gopal is the Director, Head of the School of Management and former Dean of the D.Y. Patil University, School of Management. (School of Arts and Commerce)

He has more than 27 years of CORPORATE EXPERIENCE at Bush India Ltd., Larsen and Toubro, Tata Consultancy Services and Siemens. Additionally, he has more than 30 years of TEACHING EXPERIENCE in various B Schools in and around Mumbai in the areas of Marketing, Finance, General Management etc. He was also the visiting faculty in several B Schools in the USA. In the USA, he has conducted several programs on topics like "How to Business in India". He has also published more than 200 research papers both in Indian and foreign journals. He has been awarded the BEST OUTSTANDING RESEARCH PAPER at the Asia Pacific Marketing Conference held in Malaysia. He is also a reviewer of several international journals having a high impact factor. He is the guide for M. Phil and PhD students at several universities in India. More than 100 research scholars have received their PhD and M. Phil degrees under his guidance. He is also the author of several books and is the Chief Editor of several national and international journals of repute. Additionally, he has written several books on Management which have been highly received by the student and corporate community. He is also an advisor to several Management colleges in and around Mumbai. He is also an Independent Director on the Board of several startups and MSMEs.

Dr. R. Gopal is the recipient of the RASHTRIYA VIDYA SARASWATI PURASKAR awarded by the International Institute of Education and Management. RASHTRIYA VIKAS RATAN AWARD, awarded by the Economic Growth Society of India. Glory of India Award awarded by the Indo-British Society, London, Rajiv Gandhi Education Excellence Award

BEST TEACHER AWARD awarded by the Higher Education Forum. BEST MANAGEMENT TEACHER AWARD in Management Education by the MTC Global and Knowledge Café, Educationist Award by the National and International Compendium, New Delhi.

Dr. R. Gopal received the Distinguished Service Award 2022 from IIT Kharagpur – January 2023-It is awarded in recognition of exceptional and distinguished service and outstanding contribution to the progress of the Institute. STAR OF ASIA award and many many more.

PROLOGUE

It sounded pretty remote when I first became interested in AI as an abstract topic. The more I explored the world of AI and Machine Learning, the more I realized how these tools were poised to change the world of healthcare. What had started as fascination metamorphosed into a life mission: to understand how data-driven solutions would help ease chronic inefficiencies and challenges faced by hospitals. This book is the result of that journey.

I have written this not only for the advanced healthcare professional but also for that person who has never used AI and ML and wants to understand what the future holds with these technologies. I hope the stories, examples, and insights shared in this book will spur your thoughts on how these tools can benefit patient outcomes, optimize operations, and finally result in better healthcare for all.

ACKNOWLEDGEMENTS

Many provided valuable support and insight to make this book possible. First, I would like to thank my colleagues in the healthcare industry who shared with me experiences and challenges while trying to implement AI. I am particularly indebted to Dr. R. Gopal, Dr. R. Krushnamurthy and Dr. V. P. Desa for their contributions. A special thanks to my editor, whose feedback and encouragement kept me on track. Finally, to my family and friends—thank you for your patience, love, and support during the writing process. You are my foundation.

Biography

 Dr. Balasubramanian Mahadevan, a renowned leader in healthcare management and administration, brings his analytical mind and strategic

thinking to the exciting world of T20 cricket in this comprehensive exploration of the World Cup.

Dr M .Balasubramanian, a doctor by profession, coupled with leadership and

management skills has successfully led a period of 35 years a team of

healthcare professionals in various hospitals in Mumbai.

He is a strategic, people-oriented leader with senior-level experience within complex health environments who enjoys leading and influencing change. He has a genuine passion for working with the community and other key stakeholders to improve health outcomes.In his final tenure as Chief Medical Officer at Lilavati Hospital, he was responsible for the staff's health & well-being, in addition to medical administration.

He has successfully completed the General Management Program(GMP) from the prestigious Indian School of Business (ISB)In the early stages of the pandemic, he was quick to assimilate facts and publish a book "COVID-19 - The New Age Pandemic"

In his last Book "Total Quality Management in the Healthcare Industry" he talked about the importance of TQM in healthcare and the Barriers &Challenges faced while implementing it.

A lifelong cricket enthusiast and a champion of strategic excellence,
Dr. Balasubramanian Mahadevan combines his passion for the game with his
professional acumen to deliver an insightful examination of the T20
Cricket World Cup."

Industry Speaks

Dr R Krishna Murthy

Artificial Intelligence and Machine Learning have already begun to transform healthcare. From predictive analytics to robotic surgeries, advancements in AI are no longer the visions of science fiction but today's reality. However, thoughtful insight is in order, as is careful planning and even the will to step into the unknown in the practice of these technologies. This book will be a great source for healthcare leaders, data scientists, and clinicians who want an understanding of how AI might reshape the delivery of care. The author has done an excellent job in explaining such complex concepts with lucidity and insight that this certainly will be the maiden choice for any beginner in the field of AI in the medical domain.

The healthcare industry has been in the forefront of all developments in technology. Saving lives is a key priority and the best technology and medicine available have always been harnessed by the healthcare industry for providing top notch health care.

The industry has always used top of the line technologies to reduce the time a patient spends recouping from life saving interventions or treatment of illnesses by paradigm shifts in innovative interventions, never ever thought possible just a decade ago. Changes taking place are so frenetic that healthcare is witnessing cataclysmic and mind boggling changes. The Fourth Industrial Revolution threatens and undermines traditional understanding of illness and treatment protocols. The digital world has brought us 5G Technologies making possibilities for remote controlled operations by top line surgeons very near the village or district but far away from metro towns. 5 G technologies make this possible and we are on the cusp of operationalising 7 and 8G. How ATM's revolutionised cash dispensing, remote surgery will revolutionise patient critical care and treatment. Artificial Intelligence makes inanimate machines, thinking and intelligence is harnessed for patient care and treatment. Data crunching and sifting mountain loads of data that an ordinary mind can make no sense of, data to catch underlying and unknown patterns that can make critical distinctions between life and death.

Dr Balasubramanian Mahadevan, has a gifted and deep understanding of the world of medicine and unique insights in the way organisations can deliver consistent, quality healthcare most efficiently and has several books to his credit. This latest addition to his creditable repertoire is written in a straightforward and simple language which any top healthcare professional or a layman can also understand. This indeed is a great challenge surmounted by him simply and superbly.

Healthcare is changing due to artificial intelligence and machine learning, which might lead to hospitals operating with never-before-seen accuracy and efficiency in the future. It helps the healthcare providers to mine the huge database for discovering hidden patterns, disease outbreaks, and personalization of treatment plans. This book focuses on how AI (Artificial Intelligence) and ML(Machine Learning) can bring a change into the concept of healthcare by inculcating better care, drug discovery, and diagnosis. He makes complex ideas lucid with the help of in-depth research and practical examples, enabling administrators and healthcare professionals to understand the rapidly changing technology landscape and thereby unleash AI and ML in creating a healthy future.

The early development and progress of these evolving technologies empower healthcare professionals like never before. At the same time it will leave behind those slow to grasp the magnitude and metamorphosis of traditional healthcare treatment be it radiology, pathology, and oncology, or any other specialisation

Dr Balasubramanian, an alumni of the prestigious IIM-Ahmedabad, the pioneering Management Institute has brought management insights to hospitals providing top medical care. The changes taking place provide for targeted and personalised calibrated Medicare instead of dousing a patient with a plethora of medicines hoping one would eventually work, if the patient has survived the exploration of the health care provider.

Dr Balasubramanian outlines Paradigm shifts in surgical interventions with precision and accuracy never before imagined with artificial intelligence enabling new learning in the practice of traditional medical applications. Exploring Machine Learning Applications in Hospital Settings, he explains the principles underlying Machine Learning and its practical applications in hospitals, and how data-driven insights are really transforming healthcare delivery.

Machine Learning, Supervised learning, Unsupervised learning, Reinforcement learning. Deep learning, Machine Learning algorithms for healthcare data, Predictive modeling, Patient outcome optimization and how it impacts Operational efficiency and such other concepts are brilliantly essayed.

The Fourth Industrial Revolution currently underway revolutionises Data Collection and Management for AI Implementation. Best practices in collecting and storing healthcare data effectively in a hospital setup, yet preserving data integrity, privacy and secrecy are also providing a challenge for hospital administration. It also enables predictive analytics in healthcare. Data-driven insights will revolutionize healthcare by showing how predictive analytics and algorithms can predict patient outcomes and optimally allocate resources in order to boost operational effectiveness.

Integrating AI and ML into Hospital Operations and Patient Care have been well covered. Knowing how to use AI for operational strengthening at the hospital, enhancing patient care, and developing practical applications of AI-driven solutions are well discussed. implementation not only in the hospital but in telemedicine and remote care bringing the hospital services in the comforting environment of one's home at the fraction of the cost.

Dr Balasubramanian also navigates the difficult ethical considerations, complexities and challenges in adopting AI and ML in healthcare, the bias in algorithms against the requirements for transparency and accountability.

The key challenges in integrating AI into healthcare systems, Interoperability issues, the issues pertaining to Workforce reskilling, the regulatory and compliance aspects, data quality, infrastructure, the skill gaps and finally the financial constraints that lead to ethical and unethical behaviour and conduct are summarised aptly. His conclusions and the way ahead are well researched and his experience in the medical field and knowledge of management are illuminating and benefitting the experts in the medical field as also the layman. Only a Doctor of excellence and eminence with experience in management of Healthcare Institutions could have done justice to this topic and this thought provoking and brilliant incisive analysis will help in widening the debate and discussion Dr Balasubramanian Mahadevan has started.

Dr. R. Krishna Murthy

Heading S R Mohan Das & Associates is an Advocate, Bombay High Court and Director of Industrial Relations Institute of India a NGO not for profit, non-political organisation committed to the field of Industrial Relations.

He is also Editor of Arbiter, a monthly journal published by the Institute. He is also an expert in the field of Industrial Relations and works as a retainer with Indian and multinational companies.

He is consultant in the field of industrial relations relations and labour compliance many companies both Indian and Multinational Companies

He is an NGO Member on the ICC of several Multinational and Indian Companies and has conducted awareness , appreciation, and Workshops for ICC Members on sexual harassment at the workplace

He has visited Abroad on an UNDP Fellowship and travelled to Brussels sponsored by the International Industrial Relations Association. He was also honoured on July 20, 2016 by the Karnataka Employers Association for his contributions in the field of Industrial Relations. He was felicitated by NHRD Baroda Chapter and Dr Geetika Madon Patel running Parul University on

January 28, 2023 for Excellence in Industrial Relations He may be contacted at srmdrrk@gmail.com or on Mobile No 09820303236.

Dr. R. Krishna Murthy

Dr. Vernon Patrick Desa

Artificial Intelligence is the new paradigm in health care. With the advent of ML & AI in the medical world, the quality of care will be remarkably enhanced and the speed & accuracy of diagnosis, treatment & preventive care will be vastly enhanced.

This technology essentially depends on complex algorithms which process the vast amount of data in a matter of minutes by availing of a program called data analytics which breaks down the information, interprets the trends & enables the medical healthcare provider to make accurate decisions in complex clinical situations. Dr. Balasubramanian's book focuses on the academic aspects of AI & ML whilst eliciting the various operational implications of using this technology to increase patient throughput, reduce hospital stays & drastically improve clinical outcomes. By reducing morbidity and mortality.

Hospitals of tomorrow will incorporate amazing light-speed technologies using AI which governs the fundamental principles of Predictive AI, Generational AI which leads to Transformational AI. Ultimately the medical ecosystem will be able to create **high band-width language models to perform long horizon tasks**. This would influence, integrate, and globalize medical systems, quality and cost of care & outcomes of patients worldwide.

This book has been meticulously researched and written by Dr Balasubramanian and is a must-read for every person who is associated with the healthcare industry including those in medical logistics & support services which will help them to reduce their material cost, waste of precious raw materials & reducing the exorbitant prices of medical devices. Ultimately resulting in improved productivity in the highly competitive medical industry to create an environment which is safe, secure, and sustainable for our patients. It will help hospitals to cater to daily challenges to enhance their treatment pathways & ultimately save precious human lives.

I congratulate Dr. Balasubramanian for his marvelous effort which is the fourth book in his series of medical books & wish him the best of luck in his future endeavors.

Dr. Vernon Patrick Desa

Medical Advisor, K.G. Mittal Hospital

Medical Advisor,

Sri Balaji Vidyapeeth, Puducherry,

Consultant Medical Advisor,

Accessible Health Care Global, USA

25th September 2024

Table of Contents

Chapter 1: Preface

The convergence of health and technology has opened up an entirely new frontier of medical practice, diagnosis, and treatment. Two rapidly maturing technologies with great promise for the health sector are artificial intelligence and machine learning. This book covers their intersection with a special focus on hospital settings—where the stakes are high and the potential for innovation is enormous.

The contemporary healthcare landscape is progressively marked by complexity, spiraling costs, and an aging population whose health needs are multifaceted. It requires creative solutions that ensure efficiency, better patient outcomes, and rational resource allocation. AI and ML open very promising avenues toward these ends. By turbocharging vast amounts of patient data, these technologies will be more poised than ever to create predictive models and identify complex patterns, mine actionable insights that will inform clinical decisions and streamline operations in a hospital, as well as person-centered care.

In an era where precision medicine is coming into its own, AI and ML assume a still more significant role. These technologies were never meant for the sake of automation but for intelligence in healthcare, whereby decisions are informed by data-driven insight rather than human judgment alone. This is a change that is necessary, as slowly but surely the world shifts over to more person-centric, preventive, and predictive models of health care.

It would then be all in one resource for all healthcare professionals, data scientists, and administrators interested in understanding the practical applications of AI and ML in hospitals. Whether you are a clinician seeking to make gains in healthcare, a data scientist looking to apply your skills in the health domain, or even an administrator dedicated to improving operational efficiency at a health facility—know that this book will resource you on how to effectively do so.

I will introduce the basics of AI and ML firmly and concentrate on a portion of their vital applications in health. The goal of the book is to walk the reader through the theory underlying machine learning and artificial intelligence as well as some real-world applications. Upon finishing this book, the reader will have a better understanding of how to implement these technologies in a hospital context to enhance patient care, increase operational efficiency, and foster creativity.

The first few chapters lay a basic understanding of AI and ML. We will start with a historic preview of these streams, in which we present some milestones and breakthroughs that happened in these streams and which really made them what they are today. Context provided, it is important to understand the trajectory that AI and ML have taken toward the powerful enablers that they are turning out to be across industries, especially healthcare.

This is followed by an in-depth treatment of some of the core algorithms and techniques that make up the backbone of AI and ML, including deep coverage of supervised, unsupervised, reinforcement, and deep learning. All these are discussed from the perspective of their applications to healthcare data. For example, supervised learning methods have been used a great deal in diagnostic applications, where models are trained using labeled data to identify certain conditions. On the other hand, unsupervised learning is usually applied in the clustering of patient data to form subgroups with similar characteristics that could help in treatment plans.

We also go through how vital data is in the actualization of AI and ML. Therefore, the quality and quantity of data become very important in setting the degree of accuracy and reliability of models that are AI-driven. We take the user through all the steps involved in data handling: collection, preprocessing, and augmentation. Explain why, really, all of this is necessary for successfully applying AI and ML in healthcare. Discuss the challenges associated with dealing with health data: problems of data privacy, heterogeneity, and the need for robust methods of validation.

The next step the book took was to lay the foundation for discussing the specific applications of AI and ML in a hospital setting. Probably the greatest impact is in diagnostic accuracy. Already, AI has made a lot of headway in image analysis. Today, deep learning models can analyze medical images such as MRIs, CT scans, and X-rays with a level of accuracy that can be claimed to be at, or even surpass, human radiologists' levels. We consider case studies where AI has been applied to early diagnosis, like in neurological disorder cases, cancer, and cardiovascular diseases, and saved lives by enabling early therapies.

One more significant area where AI leaves its mark on healthcare is through NLP. NLP algorithms can derive valuable information from the unstructured data in EHRs and use it to treat the patient in a better way. For example, NLP might identify trends that suggest a heightened susceptibility to certain diseases based on a patient's case history and thus allow its prescriptive treatment. We highlight a few of the many challenges associated with the use of NLP in healthcare environments, including the need for domain-specific language models and handling sophisticated medical jargon.

It also emphasises how AI is used in drug discovery and development. Bringing a novel drug to market usually takes years and billions of dollars because of the time-consuming and very expensive nature of the traditional drug research process. Artificial intelligence has huge potential for shortening many of these steps by quickly sifting through vast datasets in search of plausible drug candidates, predicting therapeutic efficacy, and optimizing clinical trial designs. We are going to focus on the application of AI to the repurposing of existing drugs for new indications, which brings a promise of much faster and more affordable medical treatment.

One area in which AI and ML have been showing much promise is in personalized medicine. In this respect, on the basis of a patient's constitution in terms of genes and other relevant factors, a treatment strategy tailored for the individual can be designed. AI can be trained from data originating from genomics, proteomics, and EHRs in order to evaluate which forms of treatments could work with a given patient, thereby considerably reducing the hit-and-miss approach of traditional medicine. We discuss examples of AI-driven personalized medicine in oncology, by which treatment plans can be tailored to the genetic profile of the patient's tumor.

Much of the book deals with operational implications of AI and ML in hospitals. These technologies will also impact hospital operations, ranging from the whole gamut of activities down to resource allocation and supply chain management. We will look at how predictive modeling may be used to project patient demand so that hospitals can get the right staff levels and minimize wait times, ensuring that resources will be available when and where they are needed.

Another such area is supply chain management. AI can help hospitals conduct effective inventory management by learning from past trends, predicting future demand, and preventing any kind of wastage while ensuring the availability of critical supplies. We will elaborate on how AI-driven supply chain solutions have been implemented across leading hospitals and the cost savings and operational efficiency benefits they realized.

However, the application of AI and ML in healthcare is not devoid of challenges. Paramount concerns are data privacy and security; health data are very sensitive and regulated. We need to emphasize the safeguarding of a patient's information when one is empowered by the power of data analytics. It provides for such subjects as encryption, anonymization, and compliance with applicable regulations in each country, viz. Health Insurance Portability and Accountability Act in the United States, General Data Protection Regulation in Europe.

Another challenge will be to adapt AI and ML into the various existing systems in healthcare. Many hospitals still have legacy systems that cannot feed or integrate properly with modern AI solutions. Strategies discussed here that have worked in getting over such challenges include how middleware solutions, cloud-based platforms, and stakeholder engagement have helped in implementation.

One other critical area we will debate in this book that has serious connotations is the ethical implications surrounding artificial intelligence in healthcare, with particular emphasis on how AI will be integrated into clinical decision-making, accountability, transparency, and issues of bias in AI-driven models. We will discuss this in more detail in light of the fact that there is an immense need to have good, solid ethical AI frameworks, with the added impetus of continuous monitoring and validation calls around these AI systems in healthcare.

Finally we discuss more into some of the emerging trends and future prospects of AI and ML that drive further innovation in healthcare. This includes discussions around AI applications for remote monitoring and telemedicine, the integration of AI with wearable devices, and the likelihood of AI playing into global health initiatives.

The fact that this book is an attempt at providing maximum coverage of AI and ML in healthcare, caution needs to be observed that this field is really changing so very fast. New developments and applications are constantly arising. We, therefore, invite the reader to stay abreast of the latest developments by further reading for more knowledge.

With this book, I hope to further research, develop, and use AI and ML solutions for hospitals. We can join hands and use such powers

of technology together for building a future where all become
healthy.

Chapter 2 Introduction

At the junction of artificial intelligence and machine learning with healthcare lies a promising paradigm shift in the ways medical services are delivered and managed. These innovations hold immense promise for bringing accuracy, efficiency, and personalization into patient care as we stand at the threshold of this technological revolution. We shall discuss how AI and ML are set to bring new frontiers in healthcare by enhancing diagnostic accuracy, personalizing treatment plans, and easing management processes in hospitals.

The Evolution of Healthcare: From Traditional Practices to AI and ML

It's healthcare that has tremendously changed over the centuries—from ancient practices that seem so medieval today to herbal medicine-based and basic surgery, finally evolving into a sophisticated high-technology health field. Deeply traditional were the earliest days of health care. Treatments at that point were often based upon trial and error, folklore, and rudimentary knowledge of the human body. These early and rather primitive medical practices, according to today's standards, laid the basis for further development.

The 19th century saw the advent of modern medicine, which significantly enhanced patient survival rates and surgical results through the use of antiseptics, anaesthesia, and the discovery of germs. With the invention of X-rays in 1895, medical diagnostics underwent a transformation that made it possible for physicians to view into the human body without making an incision. These findings paved the way for a far more scientific approach to medicine that prioritises testing, observation, and evidence-based procedures.

The 20th century saw a huge advancement in medical science with the development of advanced surgical methods, vaccinations, and antibiotics. The human body's secrets have been revealed by imaging technologies like CT and MRI scans, which have made early diagnosis and precise therapy possible. It is during this period that the evolution of personalized medicine occurred, where treatment changed to being focused on the patient by virtue of his or her genetics.

The combination of machine learning and artificial intelligence is simply the most recent development in healthcare as we head deeper into the twenty-first century. They are not only increasing the precision of diagnosis and treatment plans, but they are also transforming hospital operations to provide more effective and patient-centered care. It's the sea change toward AI and ML that is giving rise to an era of medicine in which data-driven insights drive medical innovation to new frontiers in healthcare.

Table 2.1 - Evolution of Healthcare Practices

Era	Key Practices	Technological Innovations
Ancient Times	Herbal remedies, basic surgery	None

19th Century	Introduction of antiseptics, X-rays	X-ray machines
20th Century	Antibiotics, advanced surgical techniques	MRI, CT scans, Laparoscopy
21st Century	Precision medicine, telemedicine	AI, ML, Robotics, Genomics

AI and ML: Catalysts for Change in Healthcare

Artificial intelligence and machine learning are changing healthcare—strong catalysts of change across the industry. Such technologies, by which machines learn from data and detect patterns to arrive at decisions, change how healthcare is given and produce better patient outcomes through an advancement in operational efficiency with leading innovations in medical research.

One of the maximum effects of AI and ML in healthcare is related to their potential for improving diagnostic accuracy. Traditionally, diagnosis of diseases depended a great deal on the expertise and experience of a physician, supplemented by several diagnostic tests. However, even the best of doctors can misdiagnose complex conditions, especially in their early stages. AI and ML algorithms, trained on vast volumes of medical images, electronic health records, and clinical notes, can aid physicians in recognizing subtle patterns that might easily have escaped the human eye. For example, AI-driven tools in radiology can analyze medical images such as X-rays, CT scans, and MRIs with accuracy, successfully detecting cancer, fractures, neurologic disorders, and other such conditions at an earlier stage than usual.

Beyond diagnostics, AI and ML contribute significantly to personalized medicine, which includes individualized treatment plans based on a variety of unique characteristics for each patient. In order to forecast how a particular patient could react to a certain treatment course, this would include using AI to analyze genetic data, lifestyle data, and clinical history. This would allow health providers to customize therapies towards the most beneficial outcomes. Using a patient's genetic composition to target their cancer is known as personalized medicine. AI-driven tools are used in oncology to provide such therapies, hence making the treatments more effective and less toxic.

The second high influence AI and ML have is on operational efficiency in hospitals and healthcare facilities. Those technologies are currently applied to optimize scheduling, handle supply chains, and execute red tape so that healthcare professionals could focus more on the care of their patients. For example, an AI-powered scheduling system can predict no-shows of patients and adjust appointments in real time to make sure that healthcare resources are harnessed effectively. In addition, ML algorithms can use historic data to predict the demand for medical supplies, therefore assisting the hospital in keeping the inventory at optimal levels and reducing waste.

AI and ML also make a difference in innovation in drug discovery and development, which was time-consuming and very expensive. By analyzing huge datasets involving chemical compounds and biological data, AI can rapidly identify potential drug candidates with much higher accuracy than the traditional methods. That accelerates the development of new medicines and brings life-saving therapies to patients at a more incredible rate. For instance, AI in the COVID-19 pandemic was harnessed to identify the repurposing opportunities of available drugs against the virus that would considerably reduce the time needed for drug discovery.

Notwithstanding these achievements, the integration of AI and ML into healthcare does not come without its challenges. Other than mere data privacy and algorithm bias issues, a more stringent call for regulation is needed to ensure that these technologies are applied ethically and equitably in the health sphere. Additionally, health practitioners must be trained to use AI tools in a way that enhances rather than replaces human judgment.

Healthcare will undergo a change thanks to machine learning and artificial intelligence. It can present amazing chances to enhance patient care, boost productivity, and encourage medical innovation. These technologies, as they continue to evolve, are likely to bring healthcare much closer to accuracy, personalization, and accessibility—thereby delivering quality health outcomes for patients globally.

AI in Diagnostics

AI algorithms are able to perform tasks that are not possible to accomplish with any other method, like accurately interpreting CT, MRI, and X-ray pictures. AI, for instance, has already shown to have significant promise in the early detection of diseases like cancer, frequently long before symptoms manifest.

Case Study: AI in Early Cancer Detection
A study conducted at Stanford University demonstrated that AI could detect skin cancer at a quality level comparable to experienced dermatologists. This finding gives new meaning to how AI might transform diagnosis.

AI in Personalized Medicine

In this case, personalized medicine would mean designing treatment plans applicable to single patients based on their genetic material, lifestyle, and other various factors. AI comes into play here in the analysis of this genetic data to predict how patients will respond to certain treatments.

Table 2.2 - AI-Driven Personalized Medicine

Patient Profile	Traditional Treatment Approach	AI-Driven Personalized Approach
Patient A	Standard chemotherapy regimen	Tailored drug combination
Patient B	Uniform radiation therapy	Dose-adjusted radiation therapy

Patient C	Broad-spectrum antibiotics	Specific, targeted antibiotics

How AI and ML are Transforming Hospital Operations

Apart from patient care, AI and ML are shifting today's hospital operations. Such technologies optimize resource allocation and automate administrative tasks; therefore, smoothening processes and money is saved.

Workflow Optimization

The AI-driven tools can analyze hospital workflows and recognize bottlenecks. In this regard, administrators can make decisions based on data to improve efficiency. For example, peak times in the emergency room may be predicted with the help of AI. In such a way, hospitals can allocate staff more effectively.

AI in Telemedicine and Remote Care

The COVID-19 pandemic hastened the introduction of telemedicine, and artificial intelligence played a pivotal part in this development. AI-powered systems may be able to monitor patients from a distance, conduct virtual consultations, and even deliver real-time health recommendations based on patient data.

Case Study: AI-Powered Telemedicine in Rural Areas

It can be seen in the kind of project in rural India that used AI-driven telemedicine platforms to deliver healthcare from the remotest of villages. The result: improved health delivery—reduced travel time and costs for patients. Challenges and Opportunities

A number of challenges need to be dealt with in the potential for AI and ML within the healthcare domain. The most commonly notable ones are those of data privacy, large and diverse datasets, and the possible bias of algorithms.

Data privacy concerns: Since health data is sensitive, it must be treated with utmost care. AI systems require large data sets for processing and will definitely raise questions about the security of the data and patient privacy.

Innovation Opportunities

Despite all the challenges, the innovation opportunities are enormous. AI and ML integrated with healthcare have the potential for improved patient outcomes, operational efficiency, and dramatic cost reduction in the long run.

Future of AI and ML in Healthcare

The impact of AI and ML on healthcare would only increase as they evolve in the future. Such future possibilities could include AI-driven drug discovery, fully automated hospitals, and even AI-based personalized health assistants that follow a patient from birth to old age.

AI-Driven Drug Discovery

One such complex and very expensive task is drug discovery. AI can contribute to this process by analyzing chemical compounds and predicting their effects against various diseases.

Automated Hospitals

Imagine a hospital where AI manages every single aspect of care from admission to discharge. Well, the future may turn out this way after all, as AI is already being applied in several areas like patient scheduling, medication management, and dispensing. Conclusion

AI and ML have the potential to revolutionize the entire process of healthcare today, thus providing opportunities that are second to none to improve patient care, smooth operations, and reduce costs. In light of such technologies, the challenge going forward would thus be how to responsibly harness such technologies and make sure they work in the interest of all patients while keeping their privacy and rights safe.

Chapter 3: Unraveling the Role of Artificial Intelligence in Healthcare

From its very conceptualization to the current sophisticated applications in areas like diagnosis, treatment, and workflow management, AI has changed healthcare in ways that make a difference in patients' lives and treatment outcomes. This chapter examines the evolution of AI from its early diagnostic systems for application in several medical fields today. We will try to comprehend the historical milestones and current trends that AI has brought to healthcare in order to shed some light on how it has reshaped medicine and what can be expected in the future.

Early Diagnostic Systems

The creation of diagnostic systems in the 1970s was one of the first uses of AI in healthcare. Usually called "expert systems," these were created to resemble the expert decision-making processes of humans. One of the most famous examples is MYCIN, which was developed in 1972 at Stanford University. MYCIN was designed to determine bacterial infections, mostly meningitis, and advise further on proper antibiotic treatment. Although it was never clinically applied to a large extent because of various practical limitations, MYCIN really opened the doors for further research into the concept of AI in healthcare.

The application of AI in the field of medical imaging was also tested during this time. Simultaneously, scientists began experimenting with computer techniques for medical image analysis, including X-rays. This formed the base for further advanced diagnostic tools driven by AI that exist today.

Milestones of Development of AI

Development in the realm of AI reached its peak in the 1980s and 1990s because of the enhanced technology in the field of computers and the techniques developed while getting stronger. Machine learning refers to a part of the AI domain which affirms the capability of training algorithms so that they could unveil patterns in data without going into detailed programming. This opened the gateway to AI entry into healthcare, especially in complex data analyses, such as genetics and radiology.

Major among them was probably the Human Genome Project, which was initiated in 1990 and completed in 2003. The project involved the mapping of the entire human genome. Massive genetic data were created in the process. AI and machine learning played a major role in the analysis of this data, giving new insights into the genetic basis of any disease and in the development of personalized medicine.

Another major development was when IBM introduced its Watson system in 2011. Watson is an AI that can process natural language and became famous for winning the game show Jeopardy! Yet, probably its most significant contribution has been to healthcare, specifically in helping with the diagnosis of cancer, even proposing treatment options, and sometimes predicting the outcome in a given patient.

Table 3.1 - Current Applications of AI in Hospitals

Era	Key Developments	Notable Applications
1970s	Development of expert systems	MYCIN for diagnosing bacterial infections
1980s-1990s	Introduction of machine learning techniques	Predictive models, genetic data analysis
2000s-Present	Advanced AI applications in diagnostics and treatment	IBM Watson, AI in medical imaging, robotics

Nowadays, AI finds application in most medical fields, beginning with diagnostics and treatment planning and ending with rehabilitation. Its ability to analyze massive datasets, identify patterns, and finally predict has made it a very important tool in modern healthcare.

Predictive Analytics for Disease Prevention

Data in predictive analytics is used to predict health outcomes in the future. Analyzing data from patients is where AI algorithms can identify the risk of some conditions developing in people and thus allow for early intervention and prevention.

For example, AI has found applications in the prediction of diseases, including diabetes, heart illness, and also mental illness. In such cases, AI can pick up risk factors that otherwise wouldn't be that obvious to providers of subtle changes in vital signs or patterns within a patient's history. Therefore, it allows more personalized and proactive care for better patient outcomes and protection from the associated costs to the health system.

It is further applied to monitor disease outbreaks and public health trends. During COVID-19, AI was at the helm of the fight, tracing the root and progression of the virus, predicting hotspots, and even developing vaccines. This has made this area of quickly analyzing and reacting to new health threats executed by AI in public health very essential.

Virtual Health Assistants

These AI-powered virtual health assistants will work hand in hand with patients, guiding and supporting them on their individual journeys. They can answer health-related questions, remind of medication, and keep control of symptoms and give advice according to the data they get.

Virtual assistants for health applications include IBM's Watson Health, which provides recommendations for treatment based on the available case history and formulated in alignment with the most current clinical guidelines. Another example is Ada Health, an AI-enabled platform where patients input their symptoms and are guided step by step to the next level of care.

Virtual health aides not only enhance patient engagement but also release healthcare professionals from performing linear tasks, thus reducing the burden on them. More time would be available for doctors and nurses to attend to patients, thus increasing overall efficiency in delivering healthcare.

AI in Robotic Surgeries

The other area of huge progress that AI has brought about in surgery is robotics. Advanced robotic surgical systems, like the da Vinci Surgical System, give strong precision and control during complex procedures by surgeons. Often embedded with AI algorithms for planning and execution, these systems help prevent complications as much as possible.

Some benefits that come with AI-driven robotic surgery are the ability to perform minimally invasive procedures, lessened recovery time, and a decreased risk of infection. For instance, in such procedures as prostatectomy, AI-powered robots will direct the surgeon to transmit around nerves and blood vessels, hence reducing damage and bringing higher chances of better recovery.

Further, AI may be used for the analysis of surgical data; over time, this may help to refine techniques and improve outcomes. By learning from every case, AI will be able to learn how to respond in real-time and even provide some suggestions to the surgeon, thereby making the overall quality of care better.

AI-Driven Diagnostics and Imaging

Medical Imaging has been one of the cornerstones of diagnostics for years. Now, AI is changing the space by allowing for the interpretation of images faster and more accurately. AI algorithms are developed in a way that they even beat the majority of the time with more human-than-human abilities to interpret images coming from X-rays, CT scans, MRIs, and other modalities with accuracy.

AI-powered diagnostic systems, for example, have been developed to detect diseases like cancer, Alzheimer's disease, and cardiovascular disorders at an early stage. Artificial intelligence (AI) algorithms can interpret mammograms and find tumors that a radiologist might miss, improving the odds of early identification and survival when it comes to breast cancer screening.

More so, this technology is used to enhance medical imaging quality, thereby reducing the burden of re-scans and radiation on patients. For instance, AI can help improve the clarity of a low-quality image to facilitate efficient diagnosis and treatment of patients.

AI's Effect on Health Workflows

AI offers a platform for incorporating its technologies into healthcare, encompassing anything from treatment and diagnosis to streamlining hospital operations. AI can increase the efficacy and efficiency of healthcare delivery by managing patient data, automating administrative duties, and facilitating communication between healthcare practitioners.

Table 3.2 - AI's Effect on Health Workflows

Application	Description	Examples
Predictive Analytics	Analyzing patient data to predict health outcomes and prevent diseases	Diabetes risk prediction, outbreak tracking
Virtual Health Assistants	AI-driven systems that assist patients with personalized care and monitoring	IBM Watson Health, Ada Health
Robotic Surgeries	AI-powered robots assisting in surgical procedures with precision	Da Vinci Surgical System
AI-Driven Diagnostics	AI algorithms analyzing medical images for accurate diagnostics	Tumor detection in mammograms

Workflow Optimization

One of the chief advantages of AI in healthcare is the optimization of workflow, especially in busy hospitals. Workflow optimization means that AI-driven systems may help schedule and maintain EHRs and coordinate treatment of a patient across departments.

For example, AI algorithms will utilize data from the patient flow to make a projection of peak times at emergency units in hospitals so that more resources can be allocated. This helps to reduce patients' waiting times and makes them happy; meanwhile, health providers are not worried about any constraints to deliver quality services.

Resource Allocation

Other important applications of AI include making optimum resource allocation in hospitals. With the ability to analyze historical data and real-time information, AI can effectively predict the demand for medical supplies, staff, and equipment, which in turn helps a hospital maintain optimal inventory and reduce wastage.

For instance, AI-driven predictive models can project medication or surgical supply needs based on trends of patients to have the hospitals better prepared for whatever situation that comes their way. This would not only improve patient care but also reduce costs by reducing overstocking and wastage.

Automated Administrative Tasks

Things like billing, coding, and documentation take a lot of time and, therefore, are rife with potential errors. AI is significantly helping to automate such activities, which will reduce the administrative burden on health providers and, in return, increase accuracy.

AI-infused systems code patient encounters and generate billing statements, and they can also assist in pinpointing inconsistencies in patient records. This helps a lot with time-saving and cost reduction, as well as proper and faster reimbursement for health care providers' services.

Ethical Considerations in the Implementation of AI

Though AI in healthcare promises a transformative impact, there are numerous ethical considerations about its use. Some of the issues raised include data privacy, algorithmic bias, transparency, and accountability.

Data Privacy Concerns

Massive data sets are needed for AI, which presents concerns about patient privacy and health data security. Making sure that patient data is collected, stored, and used in a way that complies with privacy laws, such the Health Insurance Portability and Accountability Act, is one crucial component.

Furthermore, there is a pressing need for strong cyber security measures to guard against data breaches and unauthorized access as AI technologies are used in healthcare more and more. Therefore, in order to ensure that patient data is handled securely and morally, health providers must collaborate with artificial intelligence companies.

Bias in Algorithms

The quality of AI algorithms depends on the data they are trained on. In other words, if the data used to train AI systems is skewed or nonrepresentative, these algorithms may give outcomes that have comparable traits. This is a concern since biased algorithms may produce differentially adverse consequences in care/outcomes among various patient populations in health care.

Dealing with this will require AI systems to be trained on diverse and representative datasets. There will also be a need for continuous monitoring and validation of AI algorithms, through which bias—introduced at the data level—will be identifiable, corrected, and reduced over time.

Transparency and Accountability

In addition, AI in healthcare gives rise to questions of transparency and accountability. Most often, AI algorithms work in "black boxes," where the decisions are based on an intricate computation hardly understandable by humans. Consequently, it becomes very difficult for any health provider or patient to trust AI-driven decisions.

One must establish trust in AI by:

Develop transparent and explainable systems. Healthcare professionals must be able to explain AI algorithms' decisions to patients and comprehend how they come to their findings. Furthermore, clear criteria for accountability should be established, meaning that healthcare providers and AI developers would be held responsible for the results of decisions made using AI.

The Future of AI in Healthcare

The future of AI in healthcare is bright, and the advances in the field of technology bring much more innovation in future applications. It ranges from personalized medicine to AI-driven drug discovery; that's just a tip of the iceberg.

Personalized Medicine

One of the most promising applications for AI in healthcare is for advanced personalized medicine. AI can help make treatments more individual by looking at the genetic makeup, lifestyle, and case history of a patient, so together, the outcomes increase while the incidence of adverse reactions decreases.

For instance, AI-enabled systems can mine genetic information to determine which patients are likely to respond to a particular medicine, thus applying more individualized and effective treatments. This has already been done in oncology, where AI can facilitate the design of personal cancer therapies against specific tumors based on their respective genetic profiles.

AI-Enabled Drug Development

AI is also spearheading a revolution in drug development, altering the methods used to identify novel therapeutic targets and create new drugs. AI will speed up the difficult, time-consuming, and highly expensive process of finding new drugs by sifting through massive volumes of data and identifying potential candidates for successful follow-up research.

For instance, AI algorithms can be used to calculate molecular structures and predict the interaction nature with different biological targets of a range of interesting compounds. This allows scientists to realize possibilities for new drugs more easily and faster. Such a possibility would make the treatments enter the market early, benefiting patients and health care systems to a great extent.

AI in Global Health

Beyond this level of individual-patient care, AI can help to meet global health challenges by increasing healthcare accessibility in areas with limited coverage. AI-driven telemedicine can connect patients in remote areas with healthcare providers to receive medical advice and even treatment without having to travel large distances.

AI can further be used to contribute to the betterment of public health by evaluating necessary data relating to outbreaks, environmental contributory factors, and social determinants of health. The information derived from this is applied in the formulation of focused interventions and allocates resources firmly towards the attainment of improved health outcomes at the global level.

Conclusion

AI in healthcare represents a paradigm shift in the delivery of healthcare services. It emanates as one powerful force that seems to cut across into modern healthcare, from its humble beginning of diagnosis of infections, to its current advancements in predictive analytics, robotic surgery, and personalized medicine. Though still facing problems, especially in terms of ethical issues and the security of data, the potential benefits brought about by AI will far outweigh the risks.

There is no mistaking that AI is here to keep playing a dominant role in healthcare, pushing through innovation and bettering patient outcomes in the future. Therefore, understanding the history and current applications of AI in healthcare will not only help put into perspective how transformational it has been but also prepare for exciting possibilities in the future.

Chapter 4: Implementation of AI in Healthcare

Artificial intelligence has been the driver of the digital revolution in many industries, including healthcare. The impact of AI on healthcare seems to be happening at a breakneck speed since changes in the methods used by medical professionals to diagnose, treat, and manage illnesses appear to change with the maturing of the underlying technologies. It offers insights into those critical areas of the healthcare supply chain in which AI is making important imprints, be it medical imaging, drug discovery/development, or personalized medicine. It is within such areas that we can see how AI is changing the face of healthcare for the better, leading to improved patient outcomes and more efficient medical practices.

AI in Medical Imaging

One of the most widespread areas where AI benchmarks is in medical imaging. Normally, images of medical conditions were interpreted mainly by radiologists and other health experts. The appearance of AI changed this process into a more accurate, efficient, and scalable manner of medical image analysis.

The AI algorithms can, as such, go through huge volumes of imaging data in a very short time, identifying patterns and anomalies which could easily be missed by the human eye. This comes to be of much value, especially in processes dealing with early disease detection, for instance, in suspicion of diseases like cancer, where small changes in the structure of tissue or organs may indicate the start of malignant cells. AI can help a radiologist double-check more effectively, be less prone to diagnostic errors, and, in this way, ensure earlier interventions.

The modern rigid leap in AI for medical imaging comes from the invention and development of deep learning models, following the neural networks of the human brain. These are models that mimic the neural networks of the human brain and who learn patterns signaling specific diseases from very large datasets of medical images. For instance, in the detection of lung, breast, and other types of malignancies, the deep learning algorithm had phenomenal accuracy when imaging via the modalities of CTs, mammograms, and MRIs.

In addition to disease detection, AI-based systems are also in use to predict patient outcomes based on imaging data. AI analysis of tumor images can be used to establish a growth rate, probability of metastasis, and potentially useful treatments to be applied. Such predictive power offers the possibility of more focused therapies, which in turn will limit procedures that incur burden and thus offer a better quality of healthcare.

AI further widens its scope in medical imaging as an adjunct to diagnostics. It is also used for image reconstruction and enhancement, especially when the image produced by the traditional techniques is of too poor quality due to either patient movement or low contrast, and much sophistication is required. Images can be enhanced through AI algorithms, thus aiding the healthcare provider in interpreting them.

AI adds much more efficiency to such medical imaging workflows, which definitely increases the productivity of the radiology department. AI systems can automate numerous day-to-day activities—for instance, the measurement of organ sizes or the comparison of images with old ones—leaving a radiologist to concentrate on other complicated cases. This decreases the huge work burdens of healthcare professionals, which makes patients wait less time to get their diagnoses and treatments quickly.

However this artificial intelligence implementation in medical imaging comes with quite a number of challenges, although many benefits certainly exist. First among them is the issue of large high-quality datasets that are to be obtained for effective training. In many cases, such datasets are not readily available, raising a major concern regarding the privacy and security of the patient's data. In addition, the black-box nature of some AI algorithms, having their decision-making process non-transparent, raises concern over accountability and trust issues around these models.

Nevertheless, the potential of AI in medical imaging is beyond doubt. Therefore, while technology advances, one can expect that the role of AI will be played even more, with already initiatives on the augmentation of the accuracy and efficiency of medical imaging, leading to better patient outcomes.

AI in Drug Discovery and Development

Drug discovery and development is infamously a long, tiring, and expensive process. It might take years and billions of dollars of investment in just the research part to finally market a drug. In this, a number of potential candidates fail the clinical trials. AI is poised to transform this process by increasing the speed of identification of promising drug candidates, optimization of trials in clinics, and a general reduction in costs incurred while developing a drug.

This is the field of large biological data analysis in which AI is first used to transform drug discovery. Researchers can use machine learning algorithms to scour genomic, proteomic, and chemical data repositories for potential drug targets and also predict how different compounds would interact with these targets. This will help identify new therapeutic opportunities which might have gone unnoticed in case traditional methodologies were to be used for the study.

For example, AI has been applied to genetic data analysis in an attempt to find mutations useful for associating with disease and, therefore, for representing possible drug targets. AI systems can also forecast a drug candidate's binding affinity to its target, which enables researchers to concentrate on molecules that have the best chance of succeeding in preclinical development. This capability accelerates the drug discovery process and increases the likelihood of developing efficient treatments for diseases with complex aetiologies.

It is also used to design new molecules that have certain properties. This basically helps the researchers create new and optimized chemicals for aspects such as potency and safety for the purpose of drug discovery. The novel molecules generated by AI are next synthesized and tested in the lab to substantially reduce the time and resources needed to discover new drugs.

The procedure of clinical trial optimization is one of the crucial, costliest steps associated with this drug development activity. Through the analysis of patient data, AI can pick the most appropriate candidates for clinical trials, thus ensuring that the study population within the trial is representative and likely to produce meaningful outcomes. Further, AI can track patient responses in real-time, enabling researchers to even change the study design if needed to boost the chances of success.

One case example of AI having an impact on drug discovery is its role in treating rare diseases. Traditionally, studying rare diseases has been pretty hard because of a small patient population and limited data. But it is in the analysis of large, diverse datasets—both in their own right and in terms of the patterns in the data—that AI has helped open new ways through which such conditions can be understood and, possibly, be treated. AI has already been imperative for finding potential treatments for diseases like Duchenne muscular dystrophy and spinal muscular atrophy, offering hope to patients who previously had limited alternatives.

Despite the level of progress made, some challenges are still being faced as regards drug discovery using AI. One of the main concerns is regarding the quality and diversity needed for data to train AI models. Generalizability of the resulting models may be compromised for broader patient populations if the data contain bias or are incomplete. Besides, the regulatory environment for AI-driven drug discovery is yet to be established; one may question the assurance of safety and efficacy for AI-generated drugs.

But the payoff could be huge. AI could speed up the way new remedies are systematically developed to help most patients, address unmet medical needs, reduce medical and social costs, and improve outcomes for afflicted patients. Those advances would be expected to put AI in a central place in the future of drug discovery and development.

AI in Personalized Medicine

Personalized medicine represents this new order of things in healthcare—from the one-size-fits-all concept of treatment to a much more individualistic approach, which includes a patient's unique genetic make-up, lifestyle, and environment. AI sits at the very apex of that transformation and further enables health providers to offer more precise and effective treatments based on the particular needs of every patient.

Central to personalized medicine is the notion of precision diagnostics, where AI algorithms make a judgment based on a patient's genetic data, a history of diseases, and other relevant factors in order to find the most relevant treatment options. For example, AI-driven platforms in oncology help analyze which genetic mutations are present in a tumor and find out which therapies are most likely to be effective. This step increases the likelihood of successful treatment while minimizing risks from adverse side effects because patients are less likely to receive treatments that are not going to work for them.

Indeed, cases like diabetes, heart disorders, and autoimmune diseases, among others, are being programmed into individualized treatment plans increasingly with the help of artificial intelligence. Indeed, artificial intelligence makes it possible to retrieve real-time information on the health status of a patient using information that has been recorded in wearable technologies and electronic health records. It can also direct fast interventions that are tailored to the needs of the patient. In chronic diseases, which require extensive monitoring and treatment regimens for optimal results, this level of customization is very unparalleled.

AI also extends not only to diagnostic and treatment planning but to personalized medicines. For example, AI has been used in gene therapy to design tailor-made medicines targeting specific genetic mutations. Both offer considerable promise in the treatment of rare genetic diseases, for which existing medicines all too often prove unavailing. AI-based personalized medicine treats genetic diseases at the individual level, giving new hope to people with conditions that were previously considered incurable. A second area in which AI is starting to make serious inroads is in the field of pharmacogenomics—the study of how a person's genetic composition interacts with and responds to prescribed medications. Healthcare professionals may prescribe correct medications and appropriate dosages, partly by virtue of AI algorithms that make use of genetic information on a patient for predicting the metabolism rate of various pharmaceuticals. This measure, apart from popularizing the success of treatment, reduces the risk of negative medicine reactions to be a significant cause of morbidity and mortality worldwide.

So, AI supports personalized medication much more than the simple rather unemotional processing of genetic information. It can also be used to build on other factors when designing the treatment plan, including lifestyle choices, environmental exposures, and social determinants of health. For example, AI might identify a high level of risk and suggest some select lifestyle alterations that could lead to better health results for a particular patient when given information regarding that patient's diet, exercise regimen, and socioeconomic status. Personalized medicine adopts an all-encompassing approach that takes into account all factors relating to health determinants, resulting in a more complete and effective form of therapy.

Although AI holds great promise for personalized medicine, there exist a number of bottlenecks that must be overcome. The quality and diversity of the data sets, which need to be representative of different populations, are primary. Lacking this data, AI algorithms can have a representation bias or be irrelevant for a significant part of the patients. Another set of issues is of an ethical nature that encompasses the protection of genetic information against possible discrimination and the infringement of privacy.

Nevertheless, the application of AI in precision medicine today is really picking up pace, opening newer avenues for bettering patient outcomes and transforming healthcare. However, with an evolving domain for AI technology, personalized medicine can only be expected to rise as a way to provide the best, most effective, and personalized treatments to patients around the world.

Conclusion

The way doctors diagnose, treat, and manage illnesses is being completely transformed by AI applications in healthcare. In this regard, artificial intelligence (AI) is improving the accuracy and efficacy of diagnostics associated with medical imaging, increasing the possibility of early disease diagnosis and improving patient outcomes. By selecting viable drug candidates for preclinical and clinical trials, AI can expedite the process of drug discovery and development in this way, saving money and time when introducing novel therapies to the market. AI in personalized medicine is headed in the direction of helping treatment providers afford every patient more personalized and effective treatment.

With further developments in AI, the potential for healthcare to get better and better will also continue to grow, opening many more chances in the field of improving patient outcomes and changing medical practices. There is a need to tease out the challenges in AI implementation: data quality, privacy, and ethical considerations—so that all this good potential can be realized within the healthcare industry. We may look forward to a time when healthcare shall be more person-centered, effective, and efficient, leading to better health outcomes for patients worldwide.

Chapter 5: Implementation of AI in Robotic Surgery

With the unprecedented rapid advancements in technology that the 21st century is experiencing, there has been an aggressive evolution noticed in the way health care is delivered around the globe. Artificial-intelligence-guided robotic surgery, this is a new departure, far removed from science fiction. Utilizing AI, robotic surgery is epitomizing the leading transformation for unparalleled precision, control, and efficiency in surgical procedures. It is within this chapter that insight into the adaptation of AI in robotic surgery, its benefits, challenges, and the future it beholds in modern healthcare will be gained.

The Evolution of Robotic Surgery

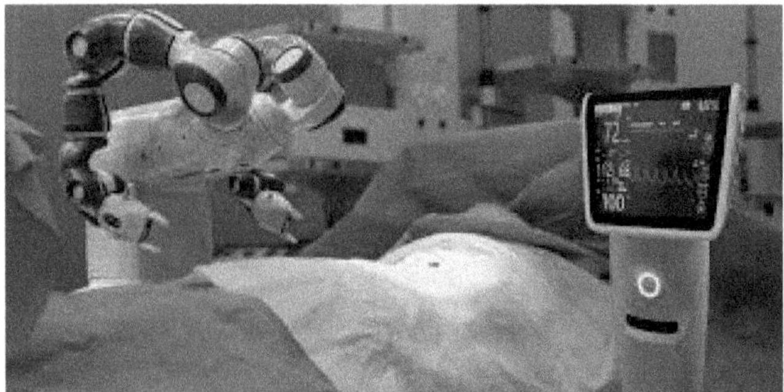

Image 5.1

There have been forms of robotic surgery for quite some time. The very first robotic-assisted surgery took place in the 1980s; however, the general acceptance of robotic surgery came through some advanced years of this decade in the form of the da Vinci Surgery System. The da Vinci system enabled a surgeon to perform minimally invasive surgery much more precisely and under greater control compared to laparoscopic methods.

The marriage between AI and robotic surgery represents only the next stage in that evolution. AI enhances these capabilities of the robotic systems by enabling them to learn from vast amounts of data, hence improving their performance over time and thus helping out the surgeon in surging decisions. This would be transforming robotic surgery from a replication of a human surgeon into one in which it analyzes, adapts, and sometimes even predicts what should be the next step in a procedure.

How AI Enhances Robotic Surgery

The performance of robotic surgery has been enhanced by AI in the following ways:

High Precise and Accurate: The AI algorithms allow the robotic system to carry out micro-level adjustments, which are almost literally too small for human hands to carry out, through surgery's real-time analysis of the data of the surgical process. High precision is important, especially during critical surgeries such as neurosurgery or cardiovascular procedures, in which even the smallest of mistakes can be consequential.

- Predictive analytics: AI can analyze patient information, such as medical history, imaging, and genetic data, to estimate the risk for complications during surgery. By doing this, surgeons are alerted beforehand about risks and can take measures to neutralize those dangers with the goal of a more positive patient outcome.

- Machine Learning and Continuous Improvement: Machine learning is a subdomain or a subset of artificial intelligence that allows the robotic systems to learn with each operation performed. Therefore, learning from experience in time allows these systems to refine techniques and become better in efficiency and effectiveness in executing the procedure.

- Augmented Imaging and Visualization AI-based imaging technologies, such as AR and VR, provide a surgeon with the most detailed view of a surgical site in three dimensions. This way, surgeons are able to traverse anatomies with relative ease and ensure that mistakes are at a minimum because of improved visualization.

- Automation of Routine Tasks: The AI will automate mundane, routine tasks in the surgery, such as suturing or tissue dissection, which would free surgeons to focus more on the complex aspects of the procedure. This will reduce the time for operation and lessen physical pressure on surgeons.

Benefits of AI in Robotic Surgery

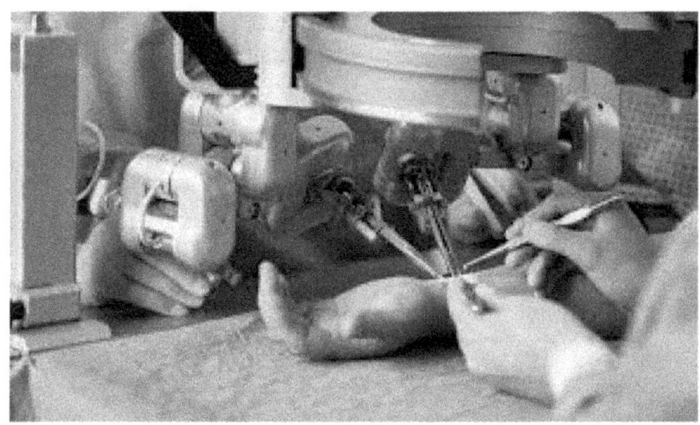

Image 5.2

AI applications in robotic surgery can, therefore, offer transformational advantages in bringing better quality healthcare to more people in the world. Improvements in surgical accuracy and patient outcomes go a long way in making the running of healthcare systems efficient. Following is an overview of the various advantages of AI-powered robotic surgeries.

Minimally Invasive Surgery

It has revolutionized minimally invasive procedures with AI-powered robotic surgery. Traditional surgery often mandates large incisions, which consequently mean massive blood loss, extended recovery time, and enhanced risks of complications. On the other hand, AI-driven robotics enables surgeons to do operations using small incisions with unbelievable precision. Guided by AI algorithms, these robot systems provide enhanced dexterity and control to surgeons for executing movements that are far more refined than what human hands can achieve.

These facts translate to several advantages for the patient. Small incisions mean less trauma to the body and, thus, less postoperative pain and scarring. Recovery time for the patients is faster, and thus, they can quickly resume their daily activities. Besides, shorter hospital stays linked with minimally invasive procedures decrease health costs and burden on hospitals, making the whole healthcare system more effective. Such advantages in turn, have direct effects on improving patient satisfaction because they can recover faster and will gain a better experience in general.

Better Patient Outcome

Probably one of the major benefits of integrating AI in robotic surgery is patient outcome improvement. Surgical precision is paramount since it is a factor that reduces the possibilities of one or more errors during any procedure. AI algorithms help with real-time adjustments, making sure all movements are optimized for accuracy. Since the degree of accuracy will be very high, there could be minimal possibility of complications like infections or accidental damage to the surrounding tissues.

AI systems can further sweep through heaps of data from prior surgeries to establish trends and risks that may arise. In view of such risks, AI can advise surgeons to make relevant decisions during the operation and hence enhance the safety of the patient. As such, reduced errors, coupled with predictive insights, result in better surgical outcomes, which means patients face fewer complications and more successful recoveries.

Increased access to advanced surgical techniques:

For far too long, sophisticated surgical care has been available only in large urban centres or extremely well-funded healthcare facilities. AI-driven robotic systems democratize health care by bringing state-of-the-art surgical techniques to the remotest or most underprivileged areas of the world in the not-so-distant future. Robotic systems like these could be remotely controlled by surgeons, thus offering expert care to patients irrespective of their location.

This can be life-changing access, especially where there is a general lack of medical resources within a region. The patient will no longer have to travel for specialized surgeries, which is particularly burdensome for those who do not have the financial means. Healthcare providers can significantly enhance the quality of care and patient outcomes in areas that have been underserved by deploying AI-enhanced robotic systems.

Better Training of Surgeons:

Another area in which the role of AI is most strongly felt is surgical training. Traditionally, surgical training has depended on mentorship and hands-on experience, which are limited by the availability of suitable cases and the risk associated with learning about real patients. These changes with AI enable one to create realistic simulations for surgical training. These simulations would be available in complex procedures so that surgeons could practice in a risk-free environment.

AI-powered simulations are not one-size-fits-all; they are adaptable to the needs and skill levels of every individual surgeon. Personalized training accelerates the development of skills by letting surgeons quickly and safely gain proficiency in new techniques. The bottom line is that the next generation of surgeons can be better trained, and hence, second-generation patient outcomes and standard of care improved.

Cost-Effectiveness

Though there is a pretty big upfront investment in AI-powered robotic surgery systems, the long-term financial gains are significant. This is the case with most AI-driven robotics, which, in this instance, trims surgery time drastically by working with a lot of precision and efficiency. This not only brings down the cost of operating room time but also gives the hospitals time to fit in more surgeries within the same time frame, thereby increasing productivity.

This also means a reduction in healthcare costs associated with surgical complications. Fewer complications mean fewer readmissions, reduced corrective surgeries, and shorter hospitalization—all adding up to a lesser cost. Over time, these savings offset the upfront investment, thereby making AI-powered robotic surgery cost-effective for healthcare providers. Moreover, with increasing diffusion, the costs will decrease further, then making the technology more accessible.

AI integration in robotic surgery offers various benefits, each of which plays an important role in enhancing patient care and establishing more efficient healthcare systems. By facilitating minimally invasive procedures, achieving effective results in patients, and widening access to advanced surgical techniques, AI is prone to make huge changes in surgery. With the further evolution of technology, the potential is huge for further developments in robotic surgery, which is a good promise for a future where everybody gets quality surgical care.

Challenges in Implementing AI in Robotic Surgery

Though there are many benefits associated with it, the implementation of AI in robotic surgery itself has not come out to be problem-free. These need to be sorted if AI has to finally meet its potential in this area:

Table 5.1 - Challenges in Implementing AI in Robotic Surgery

High Costs and Accessibility	One of the huge reasons for the criticism is that AI-powered robot systems can get very expensive, especially for smaller hospitals and healthcare facilities in developing countries. Ensuring access to these technologies for all patients, irrespective of location or economic status, is a huge challenge.
Data privacy and security	Any application of AI in healthcare requires the collection and analysis of

	vast volumes of patient data. The privacy and security of this data are of the essence at a time when cyber-attacks are becoming rampant.
Regulatory and Ethical Issues	There are some important regulatory and ethical concerns regarding the use of AI in surgery. For example, who is liable if an AI-driven robotic system makes a mistake during an operation? Well-articulated regulatory frameworks and ethical guidelines should be provided for the answer to this.
Integration with Existing Systems	The incorporation of AI-powered robotic systems into the prevailing healthcare infrastructure becomes long and labour-intensive. The healthcare provider must ensure that the systems fit well with their current technologies and workflows.
Resistance to Change	With each new technological change, there is usually a certain level of resistance on the part of healthcare providers or patients. The overarching effect relies on educating all stakeholders on the virtues of AI in

	robotic surgery to allay their concerns for successful implementation.

Case Studies: Successful Implementation of AI in Robotic Surgery

Let's now understand the implications of AI in robotic surgery with the help of a few case studies.

Table 5.2 - Case Studies

Case Study 1: AI in Prostate Surgery	Pioneering prostatectomies in the United States have been done by AI-powered robotic systems, which exhibit spectacular precision. The AI algorithms perform through dynamic data analysis during surgery, hence enabling micro-adjustments by the robotic system and further boosting working accuracy. This leads to reduced complications and cut recovery time for the patient while also ensuring better long-term results.
Case Study 2: AI in Cardiac Surgery	One hospital in Europe has implemented AI techniques in robotic systems for application in operating on the heart. These systems provide three-

	dimensional, detailed imagery of the patient's heart, enabling surgeons to easily visualize and identify complex anatomical structures; hence, they are able to avoid the danger zone. The other advantages are AI algorithms that will preempt possible complications and, therefore, by alerting the surgeon, precautionary measures are taken for the patient's safety. Greatly reducing the number of complications and increasing the survival chances of patients, this implementation has been top-notch.
Case Study 3: AI in Neurosurgery	A very prominent neurosurgical center in Asia recently deployed AI-driven robotic systems to be able to perform among the most sophisticated brain surgeries in the world ever performed. Mostly, these AI algorithms help plan in advance the best approach to be taken during the surgical procedure and also give responses in real-time during the surgery taking place. That has led to more accuracy in the surgery process, minimized risks of affecting tissues in the brain, and enhanced patient outcomes.

The Future of AI in Robotic Surgery

While robotic surgery is still in its infancy, the future for this application of AI is far ahead, with a lot of constant research and development that is set to bring about even more improvements. Areas of key focus for the future include:

- Personalized Surgery: AI will be further useful in doing much more personalized surgery based on the requirements of a patient. Based on an analysis of data about individual patients, AI can help a surgeon in planning and contemplating what the best approach is going to work for each surgery to bring great outcomes and reduce possible risks.

- Integration with Other Technologies: The inclusion of AI together with other emerging technologies, like 3D printing and nanotechnology, will only enhance robotic surgery. For instance, AI may help design and print custom implants on the go or direct nanobots to perform highly focused treatments.

- Remote Surgery: With increasingly advanced AI-powered robotic systems, the probability of remote surgery—where a surgeon operates a patient remotely—continues to increase. This may thoroughly revolutionize health delivery by opening up top surgeons all over the world to patients in remote areas.

- AI-Driven Surgical Robots: These would work independently to perform specific procedures all by themselves. Although this may give way to regulatory and ethical concerns, the associated gain in terms of precision and efficiency is quite substantial.
- AI in post-surgical care: Becoming more prevalent, artificial intelligence will allow for monitoring the recovery of a patient, with possible complications at very early stages. This could raise the possibility of more personalized and proactive post-operative care, thus reducing risks for re-admission and raising rates for long-term recovered people.

Conclusion

AI in robotic surgery really does raise the bar for health care. An AI-enabled robotic system will transform patient care and change the level at which patient outcomes can be vastly improved worldwide. This is due to the increased precision, accuracy, and efficiency with which surgical procedures are recommended and executed by robotic systems. To actualise this potential, some of the challenges one needs to consider in this implementation are cost, data security, and regulatory concerns.

With the advancement of artificial intelligence, the future of robotic surgery appears bright. This spans the whole range, from personal surgeries by remote control to fully autonomous robots. These innovations and the challenges they pose should be embraced by providers so a new era in surgical excellence—and thus patient care, even more precise, effective, and widespread—can be opened.

Chapter 6: Exploring Machine Learning Applications in Hospital Settings

With respect to fast-moving healthcare, ML turned out to be a very powerful tool; it changed everything in a hospital's functioning and care delivery. This chapter will look closer at the principles of ML and its practical applications for improving predictive modeling to drive better patient outcomes and operational efficiency in hospitals, placing ML at the forefront of a data-driven revolution in healthcare.

Understanding the Basic Concepts of Machine Learning

Machine learning is the science of getting computers to learn to perform tasks based on data without being explicitly programmed. Unlike traditional programming, where instructions are put into what must be done, ML models are trained using large datasets to identify patterns and make predictions or decisions with minimal human intervention. What makes ML well-suited to health care specifically is that it learns from data and learns over time, an inherent capacity in an area as rough and rich with data as health care.

At the very heart of ML are fundamental learning paradigms: supervised, unsupervised, and reinforcement learning. Each has unique advantages and lends itself to different sorts of healthcare applications.

Supervised Learning

Of the most popular approaches to machine learning, in general and in healthcare, is supervised learning. The procedure involves training a model on a labelled dataset. The input data goes with the correct output for the given input. Alternatively, a model is trained from an input dataset associated with the right answer, whereby the model maps inputs to corresponding correct outputs. Subsequently, after the training process is done, the model is able to predict the output for new, unseen data. It is of great value in the healthcare domain, where huge amounts of pre-existing datasets already exist with labeled information, such as patient records, test data related to diagnosis, and treatment outcome data.

For example, supervised learning models can be trained to predict a patient's risk of developing some particular condition based on historical data. Such models, by analyzing trends in the demographic data, previous medical history, and clinical tests of patients, are capable of detecting high-risk patients among them who might benefit from early intervention measures. Supervised learning is used within diagnostic imaging, wherein models get trained on labeled images that detect anomalies such as tumors or fractures. These models provide accuracy and speed in diagnosis unsurpassed by human radiologists.

Unsupervised Learning

In unsupervised learning, as opposed to supervised, the data used is unlabeled. There are no explicit instructions on what the model is supposed to predict; it is left to discover some hidden pattern, structure, or relationship. This approach is very useful in exploratory data analysis, where one aims to uncover those hidden patterns that may not immediately come out.

In the hospital setting, unsupervised learning is used in the clustering of patients based on their different characteristics. For example, patients can be grouped because they have very similar genetic profiles or clinical histories; these subgroups can then have more targeted and, hence, personally relevant treatment plans. It can also be applied to identify patterns in large datasets like EHRs, which can bring new insights into disease progression, treatment efficiency, or even patient behaviors.

Another application of unsupervised learning within the domain of a hospital is anomaly detection. Unsupervised models will learn the normal trends in data and recognize deviations that may probably point to some problems, such as fraudulent billing or abnormal patient outcomes. Hospitals are thus able to handle such anomalies in advance before turning into big problems.

Reinforcement Learning

It represents another paradigm where an agent learns how to make decisions due to its interaction with the environment, receiving feedback in the form of rewards or penalties. The objective is to learn how to work out a policy that would give maximum cumulative rewards over time. Such an approach turns out to be very suitable for dynamic and complex environments like those found in hospitals.

It can be applied in health care to optimize the treatment plan by simulating scenarios and their outcomes. In diseases like diabetes or hypertension, for example, a reinforcement learning model learns from its environment how to adapt treatment recommendations. Self-maintained, continually learning from patient responses to the treatments it devised, the model refines its recommendations to optimize patient outcomes.

Another application is the optimization of operations in hospitals. For example, reinforcement learning algorithms will learn and continuously adapt to handle hospital resources—bed allocation, staff scheduling, and emergency responses—to the changing demands posed by the hospital environment. This will increase operational efficiency while ensuring quality patient care by allocating resources where they are most needed.

Deep Learning

While deep learning is a subfield of machine learning, it uses artificial deep neural networks to model relationships in big datasets. These networks learn a hierarchy of data representations and serve as the most useful models to convert and characterize big unstructured data in areas such as images, text, and audio.

Deep learning has advanced the field of medical imaging in hospitals. Medical images include X-rays, MRIs, and CT scan analyses based on convolution networks, one of the models of deep learning, which ultimately finds diseases, tumors, and any other abnormality with high accuracy. Not just this, such models have proved to work at or even above the level of experienced radiologists, hence paving the way for accurate, faster diagnoses.

Natural language processing in medicine stands behind the massive application of deep learning nowadays. Unstructured text data from EHRs, clinical notes, and research articles can be evaluated with the help of deep learning models, resulting in more valuable insights, such as the identification of patients at risk for adverse drug reactions or predicting patient outcomes from historical records. Such insights bring up recommendations for clinical action and further improve patient care.

Table 6.1 - Machine Learning Algorithms for Healthcare Data

Paradigm	Description	Common Applications in Hospitals
Supervised Learning	Model learns from labeled data to make predictions.	Disease prediction, diagnostic imaging.
Unsupervised Learning	Model identifies patterns in unlabeled data.	Patient clustering, anomaly detection.
Reinforcement Learning	Model learns by interacting with the environment.	Treatment optimization, resource management.

Deep Learning	Utilizes multi-layered neural networks for complex tasks.	Medical imaging analysis, natural language processing.

In a hospital setting, machine-learning algorithms are the backbone for predictive modeling, optimally achieved patient outcomes, and operational efficiency. In other words, the working bees analyze big datasets to cull out critical information. These algorithms process huge volumes of healthcare data to draw out insights that might lead to better patient care and streamlined operations within the hospital.
Predictive Modeling

One of the most powerful uses of ML in a hospital setting is predictive modeling. ML algorithms, through a study of the trend of the data from the past, can stand to make precise predictions regarding future events, including disease outbreaks, admission of patients, and the course of progression of a chronic condition. These predictions will aid the hospital in taking proactive actions, ensuring better results for the patient at reduced costs.

For example, predictive models can be able to establish patients at risk for readmission. These models will use factors such as demographics, patient health history, and social determinants of health for the predictions. In such an instance, hospitals can be in a position to solve this by offering effective follow-up care or discharge planning to generally realize a reduced rate of readmission and improved patient outcomes.

The other use for it is early detection of diseases. For example, predictive modeling using ML algorithms can harness the genetic, biomarker, and lifestyle data for pointers as to what could be the harbingers of disease such as cancerous growths or diabetes. Early intervention, of course, can then be made, a fact that early detection generally allows, which usually results in improved patient outcomes and a better abatement of the system's drains.

Table 6.2 – Predictive Model

Predictive Model	Application	Outcome
Readmission Risk Prediction	Identifying patients likely to be readmitted.	Reduced readmission rates, targeted follow-up care.
Disease Outbreak Prediction	Predicting the onset of disease outbreaks.	Proactive measures, improved resource allocation.
Early Disease Detection	Identifying early signs of diseases like cancer.	Earlier intervention n, improved survival rates.
Patient Deterioration	Predicting sudden patient deterioration.	Timely intervention, reduced mortality rates.

Patient Outcome Optimization

Optimizing patient outcomes is a key objective for hospitals; it's machine learning that makes it an enabler. ML algorithms, taken from several sources such as EHRs, diagnostic tests, and patient monitoring, help identify the best treatment plans at an individual level.

For example, ML models can leverage the data of patients like yours and provide treatment plans that would be most successful for each patient. Those factors are considered in the widest range possible: patient demographics, medical history, genetic information, and lifestyle choices. By personalizing treatments according to the needs of each particular case, hospitals can improve patient outcomes, reduce adverse events, and increase patient satisfaction.

It is also applied to the optimization of medication management. For example, an algorithm may predict a patient's response to a certain medication based on his/her genetic profile and other factors. This way, it can allow the prescription of drugs with treatment oriented toward the patient and hence reduce the side effects, which improves treatment outcomes.

The ability of ML algorithms to predict the outcome from preoperative data can also come in handy surgically, therefore assisting surgeons in making the correct choices and decisions. This further leads to fewer complications, faster recovery time, and an overall better outcome for patients.

Operational Efficiency

Beyond patient care, ML is the key to optimizing operational efficiency within a hospital. Efficient hospital operations lead to high-quality care delivered at reduced costs and less resource utilization. Algorithms developed with machine learning make it possible to optimize all aspects of operations in a hospital—right from staffing and scheduling to resource allocation and the smooth management of patient flow.

For instance, ML models can be used to anticipate patient admission patterns, upon which a hospital can staff accordingly and distribute resources effectively. By being ready to respond to peaks in demand, the hospital will have an adequate number of staff and resources that ensure care is dispensed in good timing and effectiveness, improving patient outcomes and reducing the load on hospital staff and resources.

Other ways in which ML algorithms can optimize scheduling include the analysis of trends and patterns in historical data relating to appointments, surgeries, and procedures by patients. Models like this can analyze such patterns and trends to offer optimal scheduling strategies that reduce waiting times and bottlenecks at a hospital. This will bring about a more efficient use of hospital resources, all leading to an enhanced patient experience.

The algorithms of machine learning may be used in predicting demand regarding drugs, medical supplies, and equipment in supply chain management and ensuring that the hospitals have the adequate stocking of the same components as and when required. This does not lead to wastage and also does not result in shortages, which helps the running of a hospital in a more effective and cost-effective way.

ML finds application in patient management within hospitals, where the ML models can establish bottlenecks in advance by analyzing data on patients' movements and efficiently optimize the flow of patients through the hospital—from admission to discharge. That means timely care for the patient and a reduced length of stay at the hospital, which frees up beds and resources for other patients.

The Future of Machine Learning in Hospital Settings

Applications of the technology in a hospital setup will continue to rise as ML technology continues to improve. Integrating ML with other emerging technologies, such as artificial intelligence, big data analytics, and the Internet of Things, will allow hospitals to continue providing individualized and efficient care. There is huge potential for machine learning transforming healthcare, and those hospitals already using this technology will lead in providing high-quality, patient-centered care.

It is, therefore, the final conclusion that Machine Learning has been revolutionizing settings in hospitals through better predictive modeling that can help optimize patient outcomes and operational efficiency. The ability to learn from large amounts of data and make accurate predictions is giving shape to how hospitals now work and provide care in the best possible manner. As the health care landscape undergoes its continuous changing process, ML will help change the face of healthcare in times to come with innovation and better patient outcomes.

Chapter 7: Collection and Management of Data to Implement AI

In the emergent domain of AI research, data can be referred to as new oil, driving the wheels of innovation and advancement in a broader view. A hospital is where the stakes get much higher because it deals with human lives. For effective AI implementation, high-quality data, which is relevant and handled appropriately, is required in the healthcare sector. The following chapter is about the role of data in AI development, what best practices are for collection and storage at a hospital, and the ethical and security considerations necessary for healthcare data use.

The Role of Data in AI Development

Data is the crucial ingredient that AI systems are based on. In healthcare, the data can be as varied as EHRs, imaging data, laboratory results, patient demographics, and treatment outcomes. If an AI system is ever to provide meaningful insight, then the input data needs to be accurate, complete, and representative of the various patient segments that hospitals serve.

AI algorithms, particularly those falling under machine learning, require large datasets to identify patterns, make predictions, and come up with insights. In fact, an AI system targeted at forecasting patient outcomes after a surgery would require historical data depicting the profile of patients treated, types of surgeries performed, their post-operative care management, and actual patient outcomes. Thus, the more diverse and representative a dataset is, the more reliable the AI system would be in rendering its predictions across a wide spectrum of varied patient groups.

Furthermore, the performance of AI algorithms would directly depend on the quality of data: partial, outdated, or biased data can result in incorrect predictions, and such results might mean inappropriate treatment decisions in healthcare. Thus, data quality will remain a key factor for any hospital that wants to make sure AI systems add value to patient care.

Quality and Relevance of Data

The quality of health data depends on a variety of factors such as accuracy, completeness, consistency, and timeliness. Whereas accuracy is indicative of the reflection of the patient's state of health, completeness pertains to the capture of information. Consistency refers to standardization of formats and terminologies of the data across different departments in the hospital and enhances data integration and analysis. Timeliness refers to the fact that the data is up to date; in other words, AI systems are working on information which is current.

Another important attribute of the data is relevance; not all data bear the same value for every different AI application. For example, while working on the development of an AI model that would predict the chances of sepsis in patients, data regarding vital signs, laboratory results, and previous medical history are way more relevant than data regarding patient satisfaction scores. This will also involve determining precisely what data elements would be most relevant for the AI models that a given hospital plans on deploying, hence making the collection more efficient and effective.

Data-driven insight from high-quality and relevant data can completely transform the face of healthcare delivery. AI will be able to find patterns earlier, predict outcomes more accurately for patients, and may even suggest a personalized treatment plan based on data of individual patients. However, the real power of AI comes out when the underlying data is good, relevant, and comprehensive.

Best Practices for Data Collection and Storage in Hospitals

Data collection and storage are crucial in the application of artificial intelligence at a hospital level; this would ensure that data is captured in a harmonized and structured fashion, safely stored, and accessible during AI model training and analytics.

Some of the early steps in data collection include setting up a general framework for data governance. There should be clear policies for the framework on data collection, the type of data to be collected, methods of collection, and frequency of updates. For example, integrating data from all possible sources, such as EHRs, medical imaging systems, laboratory information systems, and even wearable devices that monitor patients' vital signs into hospitals is necessary.

Standardization ensures that there is maximum integrative analysis of data coming from diverse sources. Hospitals should implement standard data formats, terminologies, and coding systems, such as ICD-10 for diagnoses and CPT codes for procedures. This will not only be constructive with regard to interoperability between various hospital systems but will also maintain consistency in the data that is interpretable by AI algorithms with much ease.

Another important aspect a hospital has to deal with is that of data storage. Healthcare data can be overwhelming, mainly in the presence of high-resolution imaging, genomics, and continuous patient monitoring. The hospitals need to invest in scalable data storage solutions in order to handle large-sized data sets and provide fast access to data whenever needed.

Cloud-based storage solutions, however, have so far proved a workable alternative for hospitals in storing massive volumes of data. The solutions are flexible, scalable, and cost-effective, hence giving room for increased storage capacity as their data needs increase. Furthermore, cloud-based systems allow access to and the sharing of data in real-time among different departments or even different hospitals, hence encouraging collaboration in AI research and development.

However, the questions of data security and patient privacy make cloud-based storage important. For this purpose, strong encryption protocols should be installed in hospitals to protect data at rest as well as in transit. Access controls should be implemented to ensure that sensitive patient data is accessible to authorized personnel only, with audit trails to track who and when accessed the data.

Ethical Data Collection

Any process involving the collection of healthcare data, especially regarding the training of AI systems, should ideally be handled with consideration for ethics. That would mean strict ethics conducted by a hospital to guarantee the sanctity of patient rights and the transparency and equity in processes relating to data collection.

Informed consent is one of the cornerstones in ethical data collection. No concealment of facts should be made from the patients regarding the utilization of their data, including the purpose of AI research, possible risks, and security measures towards the protection of privacy. Consent has to be voluntary, free from any element of compulsion, and a patient always reserves the right to withdraw his/her consent at any point in time without incurring any adverse consequences.

Other critical ethical practices involve the anonymisation of data, especially for AI research. It is a process of removing or masking PII data, hence shielding the patients' privacy. Hospitals need to devise adequate anonymization techniques where the possibility of inferring the patient's identity through the data will be blocked.

Bias in the collection of data is another ethical concern that should be addressed by hospitals. AI systems are only as good as the data they are trained on, and biased data results in biased outcomes. An example would be an AI model that was trained using data from one demographic group that may fail to generalize well on other patient groups. Therefore, hospitals must try to collect diverse and representative data that resembles the varied patient populations they serve. This will not only make the workings of AI fairer but also ensure that the insights developed are relevant for all patients, irrespective of their background.

Data Storage Security

Data security is a key concern in hospital data management, given the sensitive nature of healthcare data. Breach of security can have serious implications, including loss of patient trust, legal actions, and economic fines. It is, therefore, of utmost importance that hospitals put in place tight security measures to safeguard patient information against unauthorized access, data breaches, and other forms of security violations.

The most efficient way to secure data is through encryption. For hospitals, encryption ensures that even when data is intercepted during transmission or accessed by unauthorized persons, the data cannot be read without the correct decryption key. Encryption should be provided for both data at rest- that is, stored data- and data in transit- that is, data being transmitted across the network.

Access control mechanisms are also deployed to ensure data security. Hospitals should provide role-based access controls, where access to data will be granted based on the user's role within an organization. For example, a doctor may have all access rights to a patient's full medical record, whereas a billing clerk will see only the information about the billing. In this way, by giving access to the data based on the need-to-know principle, it reduces unauthorized data access in hospitals.

For instance, regular security audits and vulnerability assessments should be carried out to detect and fix any potential security flaws. Such audits will help hospitals stay ahead of emerging threats and ensure their data protection is current. Incident response plans would quickly and effectively respond to a data breach or other security incidents in the hospitals.

Data Management Strategies

Data management is a core component in ensuring the applicability of AI with success in hospitals. It involves organizing and storing data, and its maintenance should be geared towards ensuring the quality, accessibility, and security of the information stored. All hospitals should, therefore, have a proper and thorough data management strategy that is compatible with their objectives of AI and ensures that any data should be managed in a lifelike manner.

Data integration is an essential aspect of data management. The source of data in a hospital setting usually emanates from many areas, including EHR, imaging systems, lab systems, and patient monitoring devices. Integrating all these into one system would enable wider analysis and provide further substantial facilitation in AI model development to extract information from various sources. First, hospitals need to make a greater investment in data integration platforms that can aggregate from a host of disparate sources into an integrated single source of truth for AI applications.

Data governance is also a very important aspect of data management. Data governance frameworks are supposed to set out in hospitals the responsibility of a data steward, standardization in maintaining data quality, and laying out procedures for access and use. A robust data governance framework ensures that the data managed within an organization is uniform and that it meets the required quality standards to realize AI development.

Another important aspect in health is the life cycle management of the data. Data should be managed from its collection and storage to analyses and, finally, archiving or deleting. Guidelines over data retention should be done in the hospital; it should stay long enough if it might be needed for patient care, research, and on legal grounds, and after these periods should be securely deleted.

Finally, a data-driven culture needs to be instilled within the organization. That would include training staff about the quality of data, using data for decision-making, and sharing information within the departments. So, by creating this data-driven culture, hospitals would be able to reap fully from the benefits AI would bring to improve care for their patients.

Conclusion

Data gathering and management are cornerstones that ensure the successful implementation of AI in hospitals. The effectiveness of AI in systems with the delivery of accurate insights to improve patient outcomes largely emanates from data quality, relevance, and security. To this end, it is upon hospitals to adopt best practices in the collection of data and its storage securely, and in coming up with robust data management strategies that will support the development and deployment of AI. Ethical

This also needs to be considered to come mainly from the consent of the patients and their data privacy. This requires that hospitals focus on data quality and integrity so that maximum benefit of AI can be availed and actual innovation in healthcare delivery thereby takes place.

Chapter 8: AI Model Development for Predictive Analytics in Healthcare

Predictive analytics has today been the transformative force in healthcare, as it allows doctors to find out what may be the outcome of a patient's ailment and enables them to take a call on his care delivery by basing it on data. The revolution at the very core is integrated into the predictive models using artificial intelligence. Large volumes of data on healthcare are harnessed in an effort to predict what may happen in the future, for identifying trends, and optimizing resources. The chapter throws light upon the use of predictive analytics in health, some scenarios of their application, and how the AI models get developed for performance at the specific objective of performance being the prediction of patients' outcomes or operational efficiency.

Understanding Predictive Analytics in Healthcare

Predictive analytics in healthcare considers using data from various historical sources and real-time feeds to make a forecast of an outcome. Identifying patterns in the data allows healthcare professionals to identify the likelihood of certain health events and take timely measures to prevent or reduce those events. The power of predictive analytics then makes this pattern of care change from a reactive health system to a proactive one where complications can be avoided, hospitalizations are reduced, and patient outcomes improve.

Applications of predictive analytics in the field of health are varied. It can be applied to patients' current risks for chronic diseases such as diabetes or heart disease. Thus, with early predictions, patients and healthcare providers will be able to implement preventive measures through lifestyle intervention or changes in medication so as not to allow the disease process to worsen. Additionally, predictive analytics could help streamline activities at the individual hospital level by doing a better job of scheduling resources, which would include forecasting admissions so that bed utilization and workforce utilization can be fine-tuned.

Because predictive analytics in healthcare holds the potential for improvement in patient outcomes at reduced costs, its relevance is on the increase. Predictive analytics, therefore, becomes a way through which high-value care can be provided in almost all the global healthcare systems facing a rise in demand and shortage of resources. Predictive analytics helps reduce burdens from chronic diseases, avoids readmission to hospitals, and optimizes resource use by making precise and timely interventions possible.

Predictive Analytics in Healthcare: Some Real-World Examples

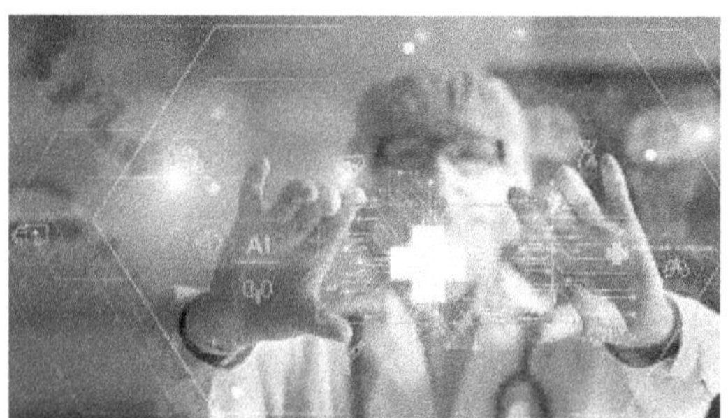

Image 8.1

Predictive analytics is being successfully used in a number of healthcare facilities, further testifying to this innovation's potential for revolutionizing the delivery of care. Among common examples of the use of predictive analytics within facilities is the area of assessing patient readmissions in hospitals around the United States. Indeed, numerous facilities across the United States have already applied predictive models to identify patients who are at a high risk of readmission within 30 days after their discharge. These models incorporate various information, such as patient demographics, medical history, and past admissions, to predict the possibility of readmission. Knowing the above-mentioned information will enable healthcare providers to make appropriate interventions-for example, follow-up calls or home visits-which will reduce the chances of readmission.

Another such example is predictive analytics for chronic disease management. Predictive analytics can use data from wearables, EHRs, and other sources to forecast exacerbations of complex diseases like diabetes and COPD in patients suffering from these diseases. Early signs and warnings include the moderation of treatment plans, early intervention, and avoiding expensive hospitalization.

Predictive analytics also continues to find its application in the optimization of surgical outcomes. For example, AI-driven models can predict the complication rates after surgery, thereby enabling surgeons to adopt measures regarding approach and preparation against any possible challenge. These models consider several factors relating to a patient's age, comorbidities, and type of surgery.

The anticipation of complications by surgeons enables them to make necessary steps beforehand aimed at minimizing risks and improving outcomes for patients; this therefore reduces the time spent in the hospital.

In the field of public health, predictive analytics has been an enormous help in several infectious disease outbreaks. Such models were applied on several fronts during the outbreak of COVID-19: to project the spread of the virus, to find hotspots, and to administer important resources such as ventilators and PPEs. These models assisted the officials of the public health department in making informed decisions, managing healthcare capacity, and reducing the impact of the pandemic.

Here are some examples of how predictive analytics have the transformative capability in the healthcare industry. Data-driven healthcare can reach more personalized care, improvement of outcomes, and better utilization of resources.

Development of AI Models to Predict Patient Outcomes

Some key steps in developing an AI model for predicting patient outcomes include data analysis, choosing an algorithm, and training and validating a model. Indeed, each of these steps is very instrumental in ensuring that the predictive models are accurate, reliable, and capable of providing actionable insights.

This involves analytics, which takes into consideration the data collection and preparation that would go into the development of an AI model for predictive analytics. Data in healthcare can originate from numerous sources including EHRs, data from imaging, laboratory test results, and patient demographics. This also calls for the most important quality and completeness of such data upon which the accuracy of the predictive model relies.

After gathering data, one must clean and do some preprocessing on that gathered data: cleaning everything irrelevant or redundant, missing data, or normalization to make the data not vary. Preprocessing is an essential phase when the information fed into an AI model needs to tidy up the information for the performance enhancement of the model by having all data accurate and standardized.

After preparation comes the selection of the algorithm. Which of the algorithms to use would depend on the particular prediction task. For instance, if the objective is to identify whether or not a patient will have some certain condition, then the algorithms to be used would be the classification ones, such as logistic regression or SVM. In the case of a goal to predict the length of stay in the hospital, regression algorithms such as linear regression or decision trees would be appropriate.

Nowadays, health predictive analytics is always at the forefront with deep learning algorithms, which can handle large volumes of big and complex data. Some deep learning models allow better realization of tasks like image analyses, natural language processes, and time-series prediction. For instance, CNN and RNN are two techniques that automatically learn the features involved in the data themselves. This would automatically enhance their effectiveness substantially in making many complex predictions.

Training and validation are the last two steps for developing AI models in predictive analytics. Training means exposing the AI model to the prepared data such that it learns the patterns correlating to a certain outcome. This includes tuning the parameters of the model in order to reduce the errors within the prediction. This process is iterative since, with each run, the model keeps refining the predictions it makes while learning from the data.

It has to perform well both on the data it has been trained on, and new, unseen data; this verification of performance is done either by partitioning the dataset into training and validation data or by using cross-validation. The metrics to be used in the performance evaluation include accuracy, precision, recall, and area under the ROC. These shall help in finding out the dependability of the model in order to make correct predictions when applied in the real world.

Once the model has been trained and validated, it is ready for clinical deployment. However, that would not be the end of the development but rather a continuous process of its monitoring and updating to ensure that the AI models remain accurate over time. This is more so in health, where the patient population may change, treatment protocols may evolve, and disease patterns can shift. Periodic updating of the model with new data will assure relevant and continued accurate predictions.

Predictive Analytics in Healthcare Delivery

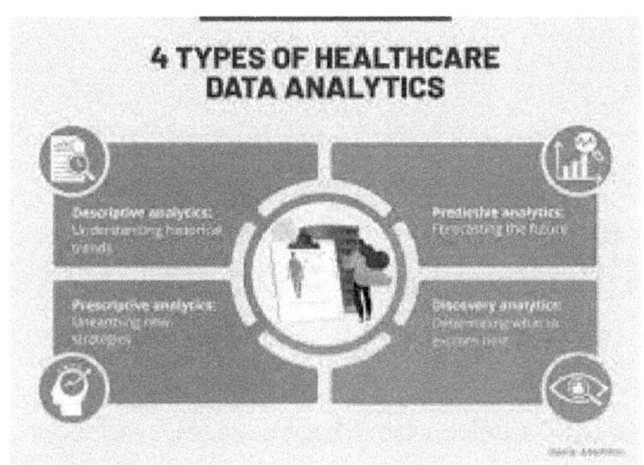

Image 8.2

Predictive analytics will take the field of healthcare by storm. The insight into patient care, resource allocation, and operational efficiency is likely to change due to predictive models.

Perhaps the deepest effect of Predictive Analytics in patient care is Personalization. By being able to determine what is likely to happen to a single given patient, a healthcare provider will be able to develop a tailored treatment plan specific to each person's needs and various levels of risk. In such a way, this delivers better results in patient outcomes and, very often, improves patient satisfaction since the needs of the patients are better met.

Predictive analytics also plays an important role in optimizing resource allocations within hospitals. By predicting admission rates, bed-occupation rates, and medical supply requirements, hospitals can prepare and position resources at the right place so they are available as and when required. This becomes critical in situations where healthcare resources are at a premium, such as in pandemics or in areas with limited healthcare infrastructure.

Apart from being able to manage better care for the patients, predictive analytics can improve the operational aspect of a hospital by reducing inefficiency and cost waste. For example, prediction of the likelihood of complication and/or readmission among patients can result in the application of appropriate interventions that will reduce the need for high treatment-intensive and expensive services. This also reduces the cost of healthcare, apart from increasing the efficiency of the general healthcare system.

Predictive analytics have the potential to enable preventive care by stratifying patients with possible chronic conditions. Early interventions by healthcare providers may avoid the occurrence of such conditions and, as a result, reduce the future burdens on any healthcare system. Proactive approaches to health improve outcomes for the patients and make healthcare systems sustainable on a global scale.

Conclusion

Artificial intelligence is going to enable predictive analytics and completely revolutionize healthcare by enabling decisions and personalized care based on the facts. Predicting how patients will fare, what treatments will work best, optimizing resource allocation, and enhancing overall operational efficiency within a healthcare setting should drive the transformation in healthcare delivery globally. In that regard, the continued integration of predictive analytics into healthcare systems will undoubtedly guarantee that the building and deployment of AI models will also fall right at the core of the future of medicine. By embracing the power of data, health providers are likely to deliver impact through more effective, efficient, and personalized care, thereby enhancing health outcomes for patients across the globe.

Chapter 9: Integration of AI and ML into Hospital Operations and Patient Care

Artificial Intelligence and Machine Learning in operation and patient care are opening a new horizon in the health sector. This technology provides unrivaled opportunities for utilizing hospital effectiveness, optimizing resource distribution, automating administrative tasks, and bringing personalized and effective care to patients. It details how AI and ML can be used to improve the working of hospitals and bring more effective treatment to patients, and it presents ways through which AI-driven solutions can be designed and implemented in a healthcare setting.

Improving Hospital Efficiency with AI

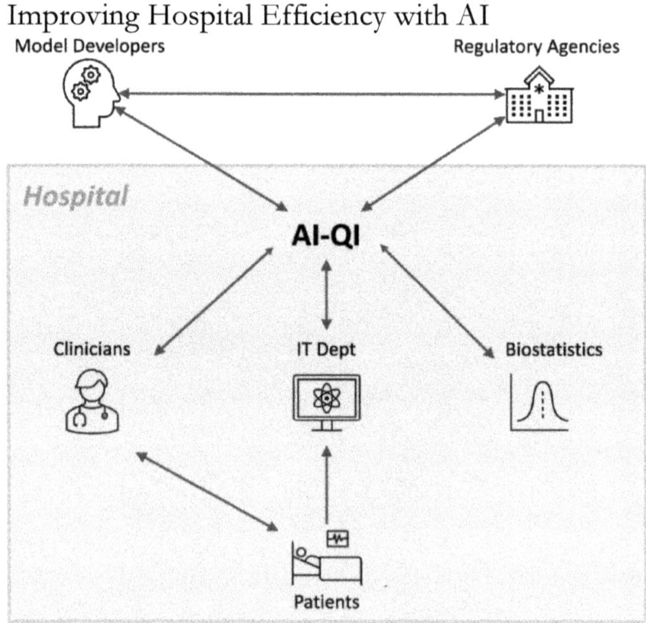

Image 9.1

AI in hospital operations effectively boosts efficiency in workflow streamlining, optimally utilizing resources, and automating regular administrative tasks. The demands for services in hospitals are increasing day by day, while their resources are limited. In such a scenario, AI holds immense potential to help overcome these challenges.

Workflow Optimization

One of the major positive impacts that AI has on hospital operations is workflow optimization. It can analyze volumes of data to identify the inefficiencies in the present processes and suggest improvement measures. For example, AI enables one to predict the patient flow within a hospital so that appropriate resources can be mobilized in place at the right time. Using historical information and real-time input, AI is thus able to anticipate such peak periods in the flow of patients' admission into the hospitals. This helps the management in managing their staff and other resources in an efficient manner.

Moreover, AI can make communication and coordination smoother across the different departments of a hospital. For instance, AI-powered platforms can automatically schedule appointments, manage patient transfer between departments, and send notifications to staff for critical updates. All this level of automation creates less room for human error, allows processes to move according to schedule, and finally enables health professionals to pay more attention to their patients rather than administrative duties.

Resource Allocation

Effective resource allocation plays a very important role in the smooth running of any hospital, and AI can contribute a great deal to this effect. Using both historical data and emerging trends, AI algorithms can predict demand with a lot of precision for hospital beds, medical equipment, and other medications. Predictive capability lets hospitals manage their inventories in ways that make sure resources are available when they are needed.

For example, AI can help optimize operating theater use by predicting surgery time and performing the scheduling. This minimizes idle time between procedures, optimizes the expensive surgical facilities, and reduces waiting lists. Similarly, AI can help manage the supply chain for medications and ensure that the vital drugs are always available without overstocking those used less frequently.

Automated Administrative Tasks

Most administrative tasks undertaken at hospitals are time-consuming and sometimes full of errors. AI automates many tasks, and when this is combined with accuracy, it can enable staff to be freed for higher responsibilities. For example, AI-driven systems can automate billing and coding while reducing errors and ensuring speed and accuracy in claims processing. This does not just speed up the revenue cycle; at the same time, it reduces the administrative burden on healthcare providers.

Apart from the manifold applications, AI can handle routine tasks on its own: appointment scheduling, setting reminders, and sending follow-up communications. In this regard, the chatbots powered through AI will answer frequent queries of patients, schedule appointments, and send reminders. In turn, less load will fall on the administrative staff, while at the same time it improves the overall experience of the patient.

Table 9.1 - AI applications in hospital management

Application	Description	Impact on Efficiency	Example
Predictive Analytics	Optimizes resource allocation	AI predicting	ICU bed needs
AI in Scheduling	Automates staff scheduling based on needs	Reduces scheduling conflicts	AI for nurse shift planning
Inventory Management	Tracks medical supplies using AI	Minimizes stock shortages	AI managing PPE inventory
Workflow Optimization	Analyzes hospital workflows to reduce delays	Improves patient flow and care	AI automating patient discharge

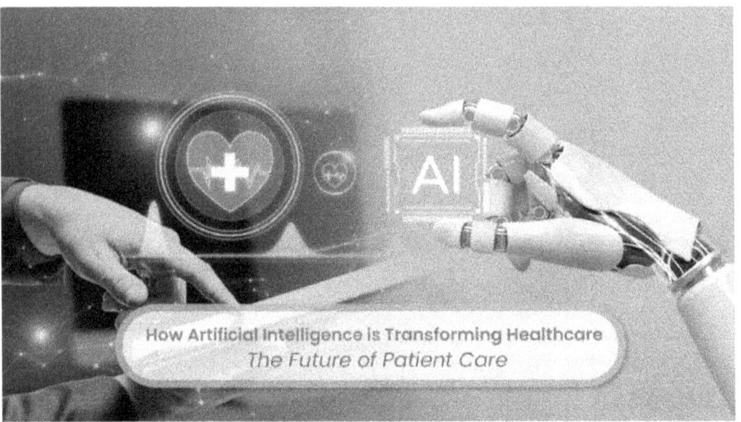

Image 9.2

Beyond operational efficiency, AI can improve patient care by personalizing the treatment plan, monitoring the health status of patients in real-time, and increasing access through telemedicine and remote care solutions.

AI has the potential to really revolutionize patient monitoring by enabling continuous, real-time analysis of data about patients. Traditional systems for monitoring patients all too often rely on periodic measurements and observations made manually, which too frequently miss important changes that take place in a patient's status. In contrast, AI-driven monitoring systems are able to continuously analyze varied data streams from multiple sources, such as wearable devices, bedside monitors, and EHRs, for early signs of deterioration or complications.

It also finds great value in the application of monitoring for chronic diseases. Continuous monitoring provides information about the progress of a patient's condition over time. For example, AI-powered monitoring systems track the blood glucose level of patients with diabetes, thus enabling the fine-tuning of the disease and its complications. In patients with chronic respiratory conditions, AI can monitor lung function for very early signs of exacerbation and thus intervene early accordingly.

AI-powered telemedicine platforms can offer virtual consultations supported by AI-powered diagnostic tools. For example, AI algorithms can interpret images from a patient's smartphone camera or remote monitoring devices to help with the diagnosis of skin conditions, upper respiratory infections, and other commonly occurring diseases. On the other hand, this would also enable health professionals to deliver appropriate diagnosis and treatment recommendations without depending on physical office visits.

Diagnostics coupled with AI, therefore, have the potential to enhance remote care through continuous monitoring and personalized care plans. Patients with chronic conditions, such as hypertension or diabetes, may monitor their health from the comfort of their homes through devices powered by AI. These may automatically relay the data to healthcare providers, who would use AI algorithms to analyze it and alter the treatment plan where necessary. This approach ensures better outcomes not only among the patients themselves but also serves to lighten the burden on healthcare facilities since the visitations by patients are less frequent.

AI can also help enable more remote care by allowing decision support. Data from such AI-enabled platforms analyzes the patient data and provides suggestions on possible diagnosis or treatment options, enabling clinicians to make informed decisions even without the benefit of face-to-face interaction with the patient. In remote areas, where specialist shortages are most common, this can help ease some shortages in specialized care.

Besides, AI overcomes certain barriers in telemedicine, such as the language barrier, through real-time translation. This might also involve the use of AI-powered translation tools so that patients can communicate well with their health providers even when both parties use different native languages, hence ensuring equity in care and timeliness regardless of distance or language barriers.

Creating Real-World Applications of AI-Driven Solutions

Key to the development of practical applications that can be seamlessly integrated into current health systems is fully realizing the power of AI, both in hospital operations and in the care of patients. This requires a multidisciplinary approach by providers, data scientists, and technology developers.

These will form the very foundation of any AI-powered solution, which could vary from optimization of resource allocation to offering personalized treatment plans for patients. Once the problem is identified, the next step would be data collection and analysis. This forms the basis for developing AI algorithms that can actually cater to the identified challenges.

The second important thing is to ensure AI-driven solutions are user-friendly and accessible to healthcare providers through the design of intuitive, easy-to-use interfaces. Equally, training and support should be provided to health workers so they can use AI tools effectively in daily practice. Also very relevant is the ethical consideration of AI in health regarding data privacy and bias issues, and the potential impact on provider-patient relationships.

Moreover, for actual implementation, AI-driven solutions must be integrated into workflows in such a way that the delivery of care is not hampered. This might imply redesigning processes to accommodate the AI tools or developing new protocols that work out the AI-driven insights into decision-making. Monitoring and periodic evaluation of AI-driven solutions are also of prime importance in ensuring they yield the desired outputs and meet the requirements of emerging needs.

Finally, innovation must be promoted within a healthcare organization. The providers must be motivated to adopt newer technologies, and opportunities for collaboration between clinical and technical teams will most definitely drive the successful adoption of AI-driven solutions. An enabling atmosphere will ensure hospitals are able to take full leverage of AI and ML to improve operations and enhance patient care.

Conclusion

Artificial intelligence and machine learning integrated with hospitals will help upgrade care efficiency, optimize resource utilization, and individualize treatment. In this way, healthcare providers will be efficiently working, automating routine tasks, and delivering more timely and precise care to the patients. Therefore, healthcare is only bound to increase in the offering of new opportunities to improve patient outcomes and change the delivery of care.

Chapter 10: Ethical Considerations in AI Adoption in Healthcare

Artificial Intelligence and Machine Learning are changing the face of health care with their novelty in solutions for patient care, diagnosis, and operational efficiency. Yet, with this technological revolution comes a host of ethical issues that need to be sensitively negotiated to ensure that the benefits of both AI and ML are properly realized without compromising the values underlying healthcare. This chapter provides an overview of the main ethical issues arising in AI and ML related to health care with regard to data privacy, biased algorithms, and demands for transparency and accountability.

Image 10.1 - Ethical Issues in AI and ML Implementation

Ethical Issue	Description	Impact on Healthcare	Example
Data Privacy	Patient data vulnerability	Potential for data breaches	Misuse of sensitive patient data
Bias in Algorithms	AI systems reflecting biases in training data	Unfair treatment of certain groups	Racial bias in diagnostic AI
Transparency	Lack of explainability in AI decisions	Reduces patient trust	Black-box AI models in diagnosis

| Accountability | Unclear responsibility for AI errors | Difficulty in determining liability | AI misdiagnosing a patient |

The integration of AI and ML in health systems presents ethical issues as a direct result of the nature of these technologies. Unlike other tools developed to date, AI and ML are learning systems that acquire skills from data. As such, they are much more powerful yet can be problematic if not controlled properly.

Table 10.2 - Issues of Privacy with Data

Data Privacy Concern	Description	Mitigation Strategy	Example
Unauthorized Access	Risk of unauthorized parties accessing data	Implement robust encryption protocols	HIPAA violations in hospital data
Data Anonymization Issues	Data may be re-identified	Use stronger anonymization techniques	Re-identification of patient data
Data Sharing with Third Parties	External parties accessing sensitive data	Establish strict data-sharing policies	Vendors misusing patient data

The most consistent ethical dilemmas in the deployment of AI and ML in healthcare pertain to the privacy of health data. For whatever it may do, AI systems need substantial amounts of data, which in this case will decidedly contain sensitive information relative to one's history, genetics, and vital signs in real-time. Collection, storage, and analysis of such sensitive information raise crucial concerns of privacy, considering who has access to the information and how the information is used.

These are protected by strict regulations such as the United States Health Insurance Portability and Accountability Act, which creates a standard in order to protect health information. The use of AI in health has introduced new challenges to regulatory frameworks such as these. For example, AI systems may require data from various sources, such as external databases, data which could, therefore, be transmitted across borders or to third parties not taken into account by previous regulations.

Also, AI systems may create new information, by inference, from the data that it handles, information that may not have been anticipated at the time of data gathering. This throws up questions of informed consent-whether the patients are aware of exactly how AI systems will use their data and whether they can opt-out in certain cases. The strong data governance framework with crystal-clear policies on data collection, usage, and sharing, along with mechanisms to exercise control over personal information, helps in the respect for the privacy of patients in the AI era.

Bias in Algorithms

The second most important ethical concern when considering the adoption of AI and ML in healthcare is the issue of possible algorithm bias. An AI system can be only as good as the data on which it was trained; thus, any biased data will undoubtedly result in biased AI outputs. In healthcare, such systems may lead to severe disparities in treatment and clinical outcomes among different patient groups.

For example, AI algorithms usually perform poorly for patients from other demographic groups if they are trained mainly on data from a specific demographic group. This could be a cause of misdiagnosis, inappropriate recommendations regarding treatment, or inequity in the way access to care is provided. This can propagate current inequities in healthcare associated with race, gender, or socioeconomic status through biased AI algorithms.

Bias in AI has to be outcompeted proactively by developing algorithms that start with representative data from diverse patient populations and are tested and refined periodically for identifying and mitigating bias. It also entails bringing on board various stakeholders in the design and deployment of AI systems, including patients, health care providers, and ethicists, enabling it to take into consideration a wide array of perspectives.

Transparency and Accountability
The two fundamental ethical considerations concerning the adoption of AI and ML in health care involve such points as transparency and accountability. Most AI systems are gradually becoming complex and autonomous in operation. This can make it really hard to understand how healthcare providers, patients, and

regulators come to a decision. Lack of transparency will result in erosion of trust in AI systems and accountability in case something goes wrong.

AI transparency is defined as the degree to which one can define and explain how a certain AI system works and by what methods it processes data, makes decisions, and learns over time. This cuts right at the very heart of healthcare because decisions emanating from an AI system may have life-or-death consequences. Sufficient trust and confidence in their recommendations can come only when the AI systems become sufficiently transparent.

Accountability in that respect involves the line of responsibility with respect to actions and decisions performed through AI systems. This not only means determining who is responsible for developing, deploying, and overseeing AI systems but who would be accountable in case something goes wrong. This can be particularly very complex in healthcare because most AI systems involve multiple stakeholders, including technology developers, healthcare providers, and regulatory bodies.

Overcoming these challenges requires the development of frameworks guiding AI system governance in health, emphasizing transparency and accountability. The latter includes standards for documentation and auditing of the AI systems, training of healthcare providers in the use of AI tools, and clear channels for reporting and addressing issues as they arise.

Navigating Ethical Complexities in AI Adoption

Success in handling the ethical intricacies associated with the adoption of AI in healthcare is multilayered, balancing innovation with responsibility. One such strategic approach in that direction is the development of ethical guidelines and standards that govern the use of AI in healthcare. In that respect, such guidelines and standards are to be developed in collaboration with a wide array of stakeholders including patients, healthcare providers, technologists, and ethicists who can assure their reflection of values and priorities within the health care community.

Besides guidelines, there is a need for constant ethical monitoring of AI systems in healthcare. This might involve the establishment of ethics committees or boards that will approve AI projects and advice on ethical issues. This could also be a body involved in the monitoring of long-term effects of AI on health and ensuring that at each step of development and deployment, ethical considerations are captured.

Education and training are also aligned with addressing the ethical issues of AI in healthcare. There is an immense need, most especially among the healthcare providers, for equipping them with the knowledge and skills that enable them to use AI tools responsibly and recognize and deal with ethical issues as they come about. This would include incorporation of ethics training in medical education and ongoing professional development opportunities related to the ethical implications of AI.

Finally, this requires the engagement of patients in discussions on the ethical use of AI in healthcare. It means that the patients have to be well-informed about how their care would incorporate AI, what the possible benefits and risks from its application are, and what rights they have concerning their data and related use of AI in their treatment. Empowering patients to be active participants in decisions about AI will help ensure that AI is used in ways that respect their values and preferences.

Conclusion

The potential of AI and ML adoption to help bring transformational improvements in patient care and operational efficiency presents many significant ethical challenges. It includes but is not limited to data privacy, biased algorithms, and transparency with accountability while making sure that the use of AI in healthcare is responsible. The healthcare community will be better positioned to understand the complexity of the issue at hand and unleash the full power of AI to improve health for one and all by providing oversight and active engagement among healthcare providers and patients concerning the responsible use of AI, coupled with the creation of robust ethics guidelines.

Chapter 11: Challenges: Identifying and Overcoming Them

The integration of artificial intelligence into healthcare can potentially bring a sea change in the diagnosis and care of patients, operational efficiency, and biological research. Yet, in the process of translation, this potential faces various challenges. Therefore, AI implementation in health is going to be quite cumbersome because one usually faces several technical, ethical, financial, and organizational hurdles. This chapter looks at the major challenges that have arisen during the integration of AI into the healthcare system, besides measures for surmounting these.

Integration Complexity of AI into Healthcare Systems

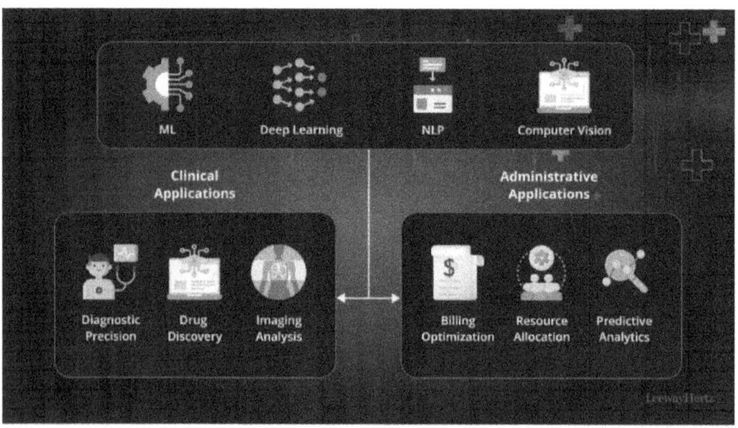

Image 11.1

Table 11.1 – Challenge

Challenge	Description	Impact on Healthcare
Interoperability Issues	Difficulty in integrating AI with existing hospital systems	Delayed adoption and reduced efficiency
Workforce Reskilling	Need for training healthcare workers in AI technologies	Resistance to AI adoption, slower uptake
Regulatory Compliance	Complex regulations surrounding AI use in healthcare	Delays in AI deployment due to compliance
Data Quality	Inconsistent or inaccurate healthcare data	Poor AI model performance and reliability
Financial Constraints	High cost of implementing AI solutions	Limited access to AI for smaller hospitals

Artificial intelligence implementation in healthcare is not as straightforward as it seems. Unlike other industries, there are several unique characteristics of healthcare which make the adoption of AI quite difficult. Complexity of data from health care, interoperability between various systems, maintainability of patient safety and privacy - these three seem to make it hard to integrate the technologies of AI. The health sector is generally a very conservative sector and usually keen on evidence-based practice, adherence to regulations; hence, this may slow down its acceptance of novel technologies.

The first key challenge relates to interoperability. Most healthcare systems are siloed-operating systems in individual departments with distinct facilities for handling patient information, diagnostics, treatment plans, and administrative functions. These systems seldom are designed to work together in this way, creating major obstacles to integrating the AI solution that requires comprehensive real-time data. With artificial intelligence, its performance of meaningful insight depends on the consumption of substantial datasets across a variety of dimensions in patient care, without interoperability in place, gathering and synthesizing that data is a monumental task.

The second big challenge in terms of AI implementation is workforce reskilling. In other words, AI technologies require a different set of skills for health professionals. Doctors, nurses, administrative people have to get used to these new tools, interpret their output, and incorporate it into their daily workflows. For most health professionals, training and experience with AI stand in the way of potential technologies and their use in practice.

Moreover, AI adoption in healthcare also brings daunting regulatory and compliance concerns. Healthcare is one of the most highly regulated industries, with endless and very strict regulations related to patient safety, data privacy, and clinical practices. Similarly, AI systems have to be compatible with these many differing region-specific regulations, as well as with those laid down within differing healthcare institutions within the same region. Ensuring that these regulatory requirements are met by an AI system is not an easy process. This involves a lot more than the merely technical considerations, to include ethical and legal issues.

Another critical issue for the successful implementation of AI in health is data quality. AI algorithms are only as good as the data they are trained on. In healthcare, data can be fragmented, inconsistent, or incomplete, which will lead to biased or wrong AI models. It may be that AI is trained on one population group and thereafter does poorly on another population group. This could then bring about inequalities in care. The quality, comprehensiveness, and representativeness of the data on which the AI is trained will be critical to ensure the development of reliable AI models.

Infrastructure is another major hindrance in the existing situation to full-scale AI integration into healthcare. Successful AI implementation requires a decent IT infrastructure, high-performance computing, secure data storage, and fast and reliable internet access. Most healthcare infrastructures are devoid of these facilities, particularly in rural or disadvantaged areas. Infrastructure upgrade to support AI can be an expensive and time-consuming process, especially when it has to be performed in already resource-constrained settings.

The workforce reskilling challenge is one closely allied to the skill gap among health professionals. As much as AI might enhance the capabilities of providers in health care, there is also a related need within the workforce for knowledge in AI technologies. Not just clinicians and nurses, but IT staff and administrators, even executives, need to be aware of the implications of AI for their organizations. Generally speaking, the current health workforce lacks competencies and skills in the effective deployment and working with AI, which acts as a significant barrier to adoption.

Probably the most pervasive challenge related to the integration of AI within health systems is issues related to finance. Many AI technologies are relatively expensive to develop, implement, and maintain; they may require substantial investment in terms of time and money. Many health organizations, especially smaller or peripheral facilities, cannot afford the investment required to implement AI. Even within more developed environments, the return on investment with regard to AI technologies is not always immediately apparent; therefore, justification of this expense is difficult.

Overcoming the Challenges of Integrating AI in Healthcare

While there are formidable hurdles in the way of integrating AI in healthcare, surmounting them is possible nevertheless. A strategic approach and leveraging on resources will see healthcare organizations sail through the challenges with ease and make use of all the capabilities of AI technologies.

Interoperability requires that healthcare organizations create and adopt standardization for data exchange and system integration. This would mean collaboration on the part of the technology vendors, regulatory bodies, and other healthcare organizations in the development and implementation of interoperable systems that can share data between themselves. For example, using widely accepted standards such as HL7 or FHIR would provide a way to integrate AI systems into the infrastructures of such health institutions. It will go a long way towards overcoming this challenge by investing in middleware solutions that can bridge the gap between these different systems. Additionally, proper investment in training programs that would give staff the necessary skills to work with AI tools is needed to support workforce reskilling for AI adoption. This is not mere technical training in the use of specific AI systems but also a breadth of education on the wider implications of AI in patient care and clinical decision-making. Partnerships with academic institutions, technology providers, and professional organizations will assist in comprehensively developing such training programs to address the emerging skill gap. It also affords the opportunity for health care organizations to establish internal centers of excellence for AI, resources, training, and support for staff as part of its implementation.

Early engagement with the regulatory bodies in the development process addresses regulatory and compliance challenges. This is close collaboration with regulators right from the beginning with the purpose of making sure the design of such AI systems will meet certain requirements in health care. In addition, healthcare organizations should establish a compliance team internally composed of experts in the AI field with legal and ethical backgrounds that would spearhead the development and deployment of AI technologies. These teams can ensure that the AI systems will not only be sound technologically but also meet ethical and legal standards within the setting of the healthcare industry.

Improvement in quality is highly essential to effective AI deployment in healthcare. Individual healthcare organizations should prioritize robust data governance frameworks that ensure the accuracy, consistency, and completeness of data utilized by AI systems. This would involve protocols on data collection, cleaning, and validation, ensuring that the data is representative of the patient populations serviced by the AI systems. The more quality the data already acquired, the more complete and diverse it could be. Also, healthcare organizations should try to source new high-quality data from sources that will emerge with increasing prevalence, such as wearable devices, EHRs, and patient-reported outcomes.

Infrastructure challenges can be mitigated with a mix of investment in next-generation technologies and optimization of the current resources to make the most of them. The healthcare organizations should re-evaluate the existing IT setup to find gaps and shortcomings in them. As far as feasible, organizations should invest in the infrastructure up-gradation to facilitate AI technologies by way of using cloud-based solutions that offer scalable computing resources and secure data storage. The sharing of infrastructural burdens for these resource-constrained organizations would be greatly facilitated through partnerships with technology providers or collaborations with other health organizations and would help in offering access to new AI technologies.

There is a skill gap in healthcare, which can be bridged through many ways: education, training, collaboration, among others. Healthcare organizations, in collaboration with academic institutions, professional organizations, and technology providers should engage in the development of comprehensive education and training programs that provide all necessary competencies in AI implementation and use to the healthcare professional. Besides formal training programs, on-job exposure of staff to AI through pilot projects, internships, and workshops should also be facilitated by healthcare organizations. This can be extended by continuous learning and innovation, whereby healthcare organizations aid in closing the skill gap for their workforce to be AI-ready.

Finally, financial constraints can be minimized through strategic planning and efficient resource allocation. Any health care organization should conduct a cost-versus-benefit analysis to identify the potential return on investment available from AI technologies and prioritize those projects offering the greatest value. Besides internal funding, there is a need for organizations to explore other external sources of funds such as grants, partnerships, and venture capital to support AI initiatives. Other ways in which healthcare organizations can make use of available resources include the repurposing of existing IT infrastructure, making use of open-source AI tools, and sharing the costs of AI development and implementation with other institutions.

Conclusion

AI integration into healthcare systems is also a very complex and cumbersome process. However, at the same time, it has huge potential for the advancement and improvement of patient care, operational efficiency, and medical research. If healthcare organizations overcome the challenges relating to interoperability, workforce reskilling, regulatory and compliance issues, data quality, infrastructure, skill gaps, and financial constraints, the integration of AI into healthcare can be realized seamlessly. Therefore, through strategic planning and partnership in this regard, investment in education and training will allow the healthcare industry to embrace AI; this revolutionizes how care is delivered, hence improving the health and well-being of patients everywhere.

Chapter 12: Conclusion

As we reach the end of this detailed expedition into the transformative potential of AI and ML in healthcare, reflection upon the journey taken through various facets of these technologies is warranted. It elaborates on AI and ML in multiple layers, starting from understanding the basics in healthcare to ethical dilemmas, problems in the collection of data to problems in integration. In fact, these recent developments hold tremendous promises, and therefore, a future in healthcare looks more accurate, personalized, and effective. Key messages from each chapter are summarized, the transformative potential of AI and ML in healthcare is underlined, and forward-looking thoughts are spent on what lies ahead.

Summary of Key Messages

This tour has started to outline the way in which AI and ML could be employed to begin with in healthcare, thus setting the scene for an understanding of revolutionary change that they bring into:. The discussion included how AI and ML powered by large volumes of data can reshape everything, from patient care to the inner mechanisms of hospitals. Initial chapters presented key knowledge about AI and ML-foundational issues, including definition, basic principles of AI and ML, and types of learning: supervised, unsupervised, reinforcement, and deep learning. Those no doubt are the bedrock upon which all AI applications rest, and any person involved either in the development or implementation of AI-driven solutions in healthcare has to be well-versed with those concepts.

As we progressed, the practical application part with regard to AI in hospitals took center stage. We discussed the role of AI in predictive modeling for forecasting patient outcomes, treatment pathways, and operational optimization. Real-life examples showed the effect in real life of these technologies at work, diagnostics being one field, personalized medicine another, and resource allocation continuous. What gives all these technologies their power is insight driven by data, since data lies at the center of how AI systems work. This ability of AI to analyze big chunks of data and provide actionable insights from them equips it with capabilities different from traditional modes of healthcare management.

The book also looked into the crucial role data plays in the development of AI. In this respect, we delved into the complicated nature of data gathering and management, drawing attention to the fact that substantial amounts of high-quality and relevant data is required in powering the AI algorithms. The related discussion on best practices for data collection and storage in hospitals underlined the importance of handling such data in an ethical and secure way. We discussed various ways to responsibly collect the data, store it securely, and manage it effectively in order to support AI efforts. This chapter also identified some of the key issues with data quality, such as fragmentation and bias, and provided insight into how these might be overcome.

Building on that knowledge of data management, we learned how to develop models for AI in predictive analytics for health. Starting with how data analysis is carried out, followed by the choice of the algorithm, training, and validation in building AI models, this chapter becomes more practically oriented in developing the AI model for the prediction of patient outcomes and optimization of healthcare delivery. Application case studies discussed the challenges and successes encountered in several healthcare settings while implementing predictive analytics and provided lessons that are instructive to those who may undertake similar projects.

Another leading theme in the book is AI and ML integration into the operations and patient care of the hospital.

Ethical considerations provided a considerable part of the book while discussing some of the challenges in adopting AI/ML into health. These included data privacy, algorithm bias, and the need for greater transparency and accountability. The ethical issues arising in the context of AI in healthcare are really complex and multi-faceted, and any decision upon those issues can be given only with much care and continuous dialogue among the stakeholders. This book gave insights into how these ethical challenges can be navigated, emphasizing the need for a balanced approach to make sure safety and trust for the patients are warranted while harnessing the benefits of AI.

Later in the book, practical issues arose with the integration of AI applications into health systems, interoperability, reskilling of staff, regulatory compliance, data quality, infrastructure, skills, and financial problems. Remedies to such challenges were discussed, hence giving a way forward to successfully implement AI in healthcare. The necessity of collaboration, education, and strategic thinking was repeated as part of any effort to integrate AI.

The Transformative Potential of AI and ML in Health Care

Looking into the insights taken from this book, AI and ML hold immense promise for transforming health care. These new technologies suggest new ways in which we conduct our approach toward patient care, medical research, and management in health care.

Perhaps one of the most compelling uses of AI in healthcare applies to improved patient outcomes. AI will leverage predictive analytics to identify patients at risk by suggesting prevention measures that may be taken, and optimization of treatment protocols will increase. This proactive health care improves outcomes for patients and reduces the burden on health systems by preventing complications and reducing readmission to hospitals. Another key area where AI is making a difference is in the precision it offers in diagnostics and treatment planning. Machine learning algorithms can analyze medical images, lab results, and patient records for a degree of accuracy difficult or impossible for humans to match, often with earlier, more accurate diagnoses.

AI is also revolutionizing how health care is delivered. Telemedicine, through AI, has made it easier to deliver health care in some of the unreachable and underprivileged areas. AI-driven platforms can offer real-time consultations, monitor patients from a distance, and even give health advice based on a particular patient's data. This shift toward home care is not only convenient for the patients but also takes some steam off the health facilities since they will have more time to attend to other critical cases.

AI is bringing a serious transformation in operational efficiency. Hospitals are organizations with lots of moving pieces: patient care, administration, logistics, and supply chain management. AI streamlines such operations via workflow optimization, automation of routine tasks, and thus ensures resources are utilized to the best possible level.

The same thing holds true for medical research. AI can speed up the discovery of new drugs, identify new pathways to treatments, and even suggest new avenues in the management of disease. Analysis of large databases drawn from clinical trials, genetic studies, and patient records allows AI to uncover patterns and correlations that no human insight could. The exciting thing is that this capability-a new generation of insight from existing data-is opening a new frontier in research and innovation in healthcare.

However, the potential for transformation from AI in healthcare does not come without its set of challenges. As discussed throughout this book, integrating AI to healthcare systems needs careful planning, collaboration, and a commitment to ethics. Addressing the challenges of interoperability, data quality, regulatory compliance, and reskilling of the workforce will better position us to take full advantage of AI. Going forward, ethical considerations associated with AI, such as data privacy and algorithmic bias, also continue to require the attention and discussion of all stakeholders.

Table 12.1 - Future Outlook and Possibilities

Future Possibility	Description	Potential Impact

AI in Genomics	AI analyzing genetic data for personalized medicine	More targeted and effective treatments
AI-Driven Preventative Care	AI predicting health risks based on lifestyle data	Reduction in disease occurrence and spread
AI in Remote Surgery	Surgeons using AI tools to perform surgeries remotely	Increased access to surgeries in remote areas
AI-Powered Virtual Care	Expansion of AI in telemedicine and virtual health care	More accessible, affordable patient care

The future for AI and ML in healthcare will be one full of possibilities. The more these technologies evolve, the more their applications will also continue to be extended toward unexpected future designs in healthcare. The integration of AI into other evolving technologies, such as IoT, blockchain, and 5G, would create novel pathways for patient care and health management.

Of the most promising areas of research, though, is AI-driven personalized medicine. As genetics and molecular biology continue to get better, AI will continue to play a critical role in developing treatments suited for each particular patient. By analyzing a patient's genetic makeup along with lifestyle and environmental facts, AI will go ahead to make informed treatment recommendations based on not only effectiveness but also the reduction in side effects. This could really drive patient outcomes and reduce costs in healthcare by making treatments appropriately targeted and effective.

AI also plays a critical role in addressing the workforce shortage globally in healthcare. Considering aging populations and increased demands for healthcare services, AI will act to bridge that gap by enhancing the capability of healthcare professionals. By using AI-powered tools in supporting diagnostics and treatment planning, AI can also allow healthcare providers to divert their attention to other critical situations. Further, the application of AI in telemedicine facilities extends health services to reach remote and underserved areas, guaranteeing that more people receive quality care.

In the future, AI in healthcare will also likely move along the dimensions of greater collaboration between humans and machines. Rather than replacing healthcare professionals, AI will work alongside them, supporting and augmenting their work. This collaborative approach will make certain that AI is used to maximum advantage, retaining the human touch so essential in the field of healthcare.

However, the future of AI in healthcare is also not without its challenges that need to be overcome. As AI will increasingly permeate health systems, issues of data privacy, bias in algorithms, and other ethical considerations of AI-driven decisions will only become much more pressing. Ensuring responsible application within healthcare means that health organizations, policy developers, and developers of technology will need to come together and agree upon guiding principles and standards for practice.

Encouragement for Further Exploration and Adoption

As we conclude this exploration of AI and ML in healthcare, let us remember that we are still at the dawn of a technological revolution. The transformative potential of AI in healthcare is virtually unlimited; however, tapping into such a potential requires further research, experimentation, and collaboration. From health organizations to developers of technology, researchers, and policymakers, everyone will have a role in shaping the future of AI in health.

For health care organizations, the adoption of AI should be embraced as an opportunity not only to enhance patient care and improve operational efficiency but also to spur innovation. While the challenges are formidable, the rewards run even deeper. By investing in AI, and building out the infrastructure that supports the technology, healthcare organizations have the potential to position themselves at the leading edge of this technological revolution.

The future of AI in healthcare promises exciting times of innovation for the researcher and developer. The next wave of advancements in health care would be further development of algorithms, models, and applications of AI. Expanding the boundaries of possibilities with AI allows the researcher and developer to play a role in improved patient outcomes, advanced medical research, and transformed healthcare delivery.

Policymakers also play a critical role in the enactment of necessary measures that make the adoption of AI into health both responsible and ethical. In other words, this means regulations and guidelines around balancing innovation with the need to protect patient privacy, safety, and fairness of AI systems. Such supportive regulatory environments created by policymakers would foster responsible adoption of AI in health.

Finally, there needs to be an increase in investigations and adoptions of AI and ML into healthcare. The journey is not without its challenges, but the potential benefits cannot be ignored for AI in health. Some next steps forward are continued explorations in novel applications and addressing identified challenges, building on successes so far achieved.

The transformative possibilities of AI and ML in the healthcare industry are immense. These technologies present a great avenue to innovate patient care, enhance operational efficiency, and bring innovation into medical research. While the journey has just begun, the future of AI in healthcare is full of possibilities. By embracing AI and ML, we can create a future wherein health is more precise, personalized, and accessible to all. Now is the time for exploration, adoption, and innovation.

EPILOGUE

As AI continues to evolve, we stand at the threshold of a healthcare revolution. This vision has been illustrated with examples of the use of Machine Learning, predictive analytics, and robotic assistance in patient care. But most importantly, we must remember that technology will not solve all the problems. The future of health is not with data, algorithms, and automation but with clinicians and healthcare professionals who adapt and learn to use these tools. Ethical questions, challenges, and potential brought about by AI call for caution, curiosity, and courage. Well, this is just the start. As we forge ahead, I hope that each healthcare professional, data scientist, and policymaker will keep asking the hard questions and working towards a future wherein technology and humanity go hand in hand to provide the most optimal care.

References

1. https://www.ncbi.nlm.nih.gov/pmc/articles/PMC6616181/#:~:text=It%20can%20be%20used%20for,management%20and%20medical%20records%20management.&text=Some%20healthcare%20organisations%20have%20also,health%20conditions%20and%20poor%20usability.&text=Another%20AI%20technology%20with%20relevance,data%2Dmatching%20and%20claims%20audits.

2. https://www.foreseemed.com/artificial-intelligence-in-healthcare#:~:text=The%20Benefits%20of%20AI%20in%20Healthcare&text=AI%20for%20healthcare%20offers%20the,predicting%20outcomes%2C%20and%20recommending%20treatments.

3. https://www.ncbi.nlm.nih.gov/pmc/articles/PMC9738234/

4. https://www.aidoc.com/learn/blog/ai-in-healthcare-the-ultimate-guide/

5. https://www.ncbi.nlm.nih.gov/pmc/articles/PMC10907451/#:~:text=AI%20modeling%20is%20allowing%20surgeons,the%20field%20of%20surgical%20education.

6. https://www.imperial.ac.uk/news/200673/application-artificial-intelligence-ai-surgery/#:~:text=AI%20for%20surgical%20robotics,4)%20human%E2%80%93robot%20interaction.

7. https://www.hpe.com/in/en/what-is/ai-data-management.html#:~:text=It%20includes%20all%20the%20procedures,changes%20and%20make%20proactive%20decisions.

8. https://www.wipro.com/analytics/leveraging-ai-predictive-analytics-in-healthcare/#:~:text=AI%2d Powered%20 predictive%20analytics%20 can,extrapolating%20needs%20 from%20 patient%20data.

9. https://books.google.co.in/books?hl=en&lr=&id=5GJjE AAAQBAJ&oi=fnd&pg=PP1&dq=Building+AI+Models +for+Predictive+Analytics+in+Healthcare&ots=MMJTO CIRjR&sig=Ny87UgVfoodY8Y2RpEtjGPNnUx8

10. https://www.ncbi.nlm.nih.gov/pmc/articles/PMC661618 1/

Verses Kindler Publication

Verses Kindler Publication

Reach us through our website -
https://www.verseskindlerpublication.com/
For more information visit our Instagram or Facebook page.